DANCE

Your Way To The Top!

Feminine Leadership without burning out

Susie Heath

Dance Your Way To The Top

First published in 2015 by
Panoma Press Ltd.
48 St Vincent Drive, St Albans, Herts, AL1 5SJ, UK
info@panomapress.com
www.panomapress.com

Book layout by Charlotte Mouncey.

Printed on acid-free paper from managed forests.

ISBN 978-1-909623-90-3

Praise for Dance Your Way to the Top!

"This is a must-read for any person looking to release the powerful combination of distinct female leadership traits and their true nature – something that this 21st century is craving for. Susie guides you through a series of easy-to-follow steps that are both educational and transformational. Whether you are female or male, this book is a joy to read."

Manj Weerasekera, Co-author of the best-selling book 'Transform' & author of the forthcoming book 'The Divorced Man's Guide To Finding Mrs. Right' www.manjw.com

"I have very much enjoyed reading this book. I found myself saying 'yes, yes, yes,' and nodding as I read. In fact I could not put it down. Every chapter led me on to more information that I wanted, and more resonance, also leading me to look at myself and where I was and what I wanted. I found the exercises useful, not always easy to complete but they moved me on at every stage. This is a book that I shall be returning to over and over again, I can see it being well used, underlined, highlighted and annotated. To all women out there, get yourself a copy because you need to read this."

Heather Waring - Director Your Virtual Book Tour www.yourvirtualbooktour.com

"This book is one of the most powerful calls to action I have ever encountered. Susie Heath invites men and women to come together, heads and logic with heart and intuition, to save our world from the devastating destruction it is currently experiencing. Susie addresses what she calls 'a deep ache in the heart', a desire to change the world, to make it a safer, healthier place to live. As she says, women are programmed to keep social harmony, so if we want world peace, we need more women leaders! A woman from my own heart, she asserts: "True leadership is an inside job." Susie helps her readers to better understand themselves in order to become aware of their unique gifts. She helps them to follow their vision whilst staying connected to their feminine energy in order to avoid burn out. I was left wanting to experience one of Susie's workshops. I would recommend Dance your Way to the Top! to ANY woman who under values her feminine qualities and to ANYONE wanting to become a leader."

Francesca Gordon-Smith, Trainer in Vocal Empowerment and Positive Mindset www.positivevoice.co.uk

"*This practical guide is essential reading for men as well as women. Beautifully written, Susie sweeps you up under her wing and shows you the tools and mindset that are now required so that we can thrive inside as well as outside of our workplace. Her knowledge, wisdom and warmth shines through and you sense that she really cares about each and every reader.*"

Prue Nichols, Wellbeing specialist and author of 'The Natural Laws of Work' - how to stay cool, calm and collected in the office. www.Pruenichols.com

"*An absolute must-read. I hear and use the word leadership all the time because that's one of my passions. And Susie's latest book blew me away ...and in the best way possible. This book is written from the heart, and leadership in this day and age has got to be from the heart. I believe that this is the era for us women to take the lead; this book talks about all the reasons why this should be the case. It cuts through all the noise and says it as it is. It is a no bulls**t, in your face book and I love it. My favourite part of the book is the section on 'Feminine Addictions'. Do yourself a favour and read it. If you want to find yourself, be bold and do something about it.*"

Anoushka Gungadin, Leadership coach-speaker. Best selling author
www.anoushkagungadin.com

"*Imagine feeling so comfortable in your own skin that you feel good saying 'yes' or 'no'. You know yourself and your needs so well that you are happy to support them, knowing that by doing so you powerfully guide those around you. That's what Susie's new book teaches you to do. She lovingly challenges age-old beliefs that are not supporting today's woman nor our communities, and shares simple ways to create authentic leadership as a woman.*"

Jules Wyman Lead Coach at Positive Belief www.positive-belief.co.uk

"*Susie's profound observations provide a mirror. Her enlightened perspective, tools and techniques are geared towards enriching your self-esteem, self-confidence and having better relationships. They are a true revolution of thinking and being. This book does not provide you with a metaphor for becoming a 'man in a frock', it supports you in being recognised as your true and beautiful self, helping you move, think and use language in a more empowering way, ensuring that you are taken seriously in the corporate world. A must-read for women who want to express their authentic self and be the leader rather than the follower.*"

Deborah Cooper, Vice President - Global Regulatory Affairs GENPACT Pharmalink

"A fresh and much-needed approach to female success. With her rallying cry of 'Why be a second-rate man when you can be a first-rate woman?' Susie Heath explores what it really means to be a woman, helping the reader lose any masks she might have been wearing and dance her way back into her authentic and powerful self. Crammed full of exercises, Susie's passion for dancing shines from the page. Reading this book made me feel inspired and empowered and so excited to be a woman. It also made me kick off my shoes and dance!"

Siobhan Curham, author, coach and motivational speaker. www.siobhancurham.co.uk

"Susie's book is a thoroughly enjoyable read. Her delightful, bright feminine energy shines through her writing and insights. She courageously combines her personal narrative with insights for how women today can indeed change the world. Her book is a clarion call to action and that's a mission very dear to my own heart. I know thousands of women across the planet who hunger for a greater role and for their voices to be heard. Susie nails so many of the reasons why women do actually hold themselves back. She reaches into her extensive practical knowledge of helping people reconnect with their innate power, to offer a way forward. I think women will find this book immensely powerful."

Gina Lazenby, editor of Feminine Leadership Today, author of 'The Rise of the Feminine'

"This book is what women globally have been waiting for! Susie describes with eloquence and great accuracy what women are feeling in their hearts at this time in our evolution. Written for women like you and me who are being called to make a difference in the world - yet continue to struggle with the disproportion of feminine and masculine energy that has been indoctrinated into us from birth. Susie's wisdom helps you to see a new paradigm for what it is. One that will enable you to ask the relevant questions to release what no longer serves you in order for you to step boldly, proudly and fully into revealing the woman you were truly born to be. Captured and expressed in an easy read, this practical book filled with powerful exercises will warm your soul."

Allison Marlowe, Founder Global Winning Women www.globalwinningwomen.com

"This book captures a new and influential message for women – and men – and shines a light on the possibility that women can lead us to a new world using their true feminine consciousness. After 25 years of research and facilitation in the field of 'gender intelligence and gender dynamics', my work has shown me that we (women) cannot achieve all we desire if we don't embrace who we are

inside and out. I encourage all women to read and act on the lessons in this book and for men to read this to be sure they don't get left behind!

I have known Susie for over 25 years and observed her dedication to being a truly feminine woman of substance, sensitivity and courage. She graduates here to her full wisdom. I love her words 'True leadership is an inside job.' I applaud her and dance along with her."

Dr Pauline Teresa Crawford, Gender Dynamics Expert, Performance Consultant, & Business Psychologist. CEO Corporate Heart Ltd UK, and President of the World Association of Visioneers & Entreprenologists (WAVE) www.corporateheart.co.uk www.worldvisioneers.org

"I have known Susie for over half a decade now both on a personal and professional basis. She is one of only a few women speakers-teachers-coaches in this country who has the ability to truly move her audience rapidly into their core energies. She does this with grace and elegance. Her style of teaching is immediately infectious and most importantly to me and to anyone in her presence - she is authentic. Her feminine energy and radiance creates a wonderful environment for those she is teaching to relax and let go. I have witnessed her move both women and men rapidly and effectively. Equally, her grace and ease in teaching allows women to open up in a way that they have never done before. When the opportunity arises, I will always have Susie come speak with me as I know the positive impact she has on my audiences."

Dr. Rohan Weerasinghe – Author, professional speaker and trainer

"Susie Heath's important book is a must-read for working men and women. The book is a practical guide for women to enhance and retain their feminine power by using all the unique feminine talents of emotional heart-centred leadership - the type of leadership that is now essential for success and survival in 21st century business. If you wish to enhance your career this book gives you all the tools you need. It is in the harmony of employing both the male and female brain talents that real success for business is achieved. The world needs the female brain talents like never before. The survival of our planet rests on employing feminine wisdom to provide novel solutions to the many challenges we face. Congratulations on writing such a profound and important book that will transform how we lead, how we think, and bring much needed positive change to the business world."

Dr Anne Moir. Neuropsychologist and author of the best selling book, 'Brainsex – Real Difference Between Men and Women'

"Susie Heath's new book is infused with clarity, insight and womanly wisdom from one who knows. Susie opens us to a new paradigm of Feminine Leadership - one where the pain of burnout, playing small, or sacrificing who you are as a woman to be a successful leader, is a thing of the past.

I've been practising and teaching women's work for decades now and I can honestly say with hand on heart, that there's nothing else out there like this!

I love this book and highly recommend you follow the transformational roadmap Susie has provided, so you can embody your true power as a feminine leader, give your gifts to the world, and be richly rewarded for it."

Lisa Page, Author, Speaker, Intimacy & Relationship Coach, Poet, Women's Empowerment Catalyst & Intimate Conversationalist LisaPage.com.au www.SoulSatisfactionForWomen.com

"If you are a woman and you feel that there is more of you to emerge, that somehow the stresses and strains of life are overwhelming you, if you are a woman whether in youth or in later life and you know in the depths of your being that something is missing, that your body is crying out for energy and vitality, that your heart is yearning and your mind is searching for meaning, if you are a woman aching for Love and 'to come home' to yourself, READ THIS BOOK! There is something for EVERYONE in Susie Heath's heartfelt outpouring of hard-won experience, reflection and advice. And this is a book for men as much as for women. My advice is simple: let this be a book to adorn your bookshelves – own it, read it, treasure it, enjoy it and above all share it."

Dr. Kim A. Jobst MA DM MRCP MFHom - Consultant Physician and Medical Homoeopath. Founding Editor - The Journal of Alternative and Complementary Medicine: Research on Paradigm, Practice and Policy. www.functionalshift.com

"This material really works, and is so relevant for the times we are living in. As founder of One of Many and the One Woman Conference, I invited Susie to co-create some of the material and co-present with me on stage. Her wisdom in general, and perspectives on the Feminine Archetypes in particular has been fundamental to the growth our clients experience. Her dance has been absolutely life-changing for the women involved. Miss this at your peril!"

Dr. Joanna Martin. Speaker and Lifestyle Design Specialist. Founder www.oneofmany.co.uk

"Give, give, give - what is the point of having experience,
knowledge, or talent if I don't give it away?
Of having stories if I don't tell them to others?
Of having wealth if I don't share it?
I don't intend to be cremated with any of it!
It is in giving that I connect with others,
with the world, and with the Divine."

Isabel Allende

Reprinted with kind permission of Isabel Allende. www.IsabelAllende.com

Acknowledgements

No book can ever be written or created without the help and support of so many people who have contributed to my life since the day I arrived on this planet – the thousands of authors I have read, all the teachers, healers, coaches, work colleagues and clients who have been part of my journey in so many different ways. Writing can be a lonely task and I'm so grateful to all my wonderful friends who have taken me out of solitary confinement and invited me on trips, holidays and seminars, who have fed and watered me along the way, and inspired me to keep going when I've felt like giving up, particularly while I was caring for my mother during her final months.

Grateful thanks in particular to Deborah Cooper for her insights into corporate life; Daniel Priestley, founder of Key Person of Influence who never gave up on me, and to all my KPI colleagues who are so magnificently becoming leaders in the world in their own unique ways; Manj Weerasekera who kindly gave me permission to 'borrow' some of his material to integrate with my own in the chapters, 'Becoming the Mistress of Your Mind' and 'Dancing Backwards in High Heels;' Dr. Tony Quinn for the Educo Mind System; Harun Rabbani who entrusted me with my own radio show, The Essence, on www.untangledfm.com where I conversed with so many amazing leaders in their field; Janet Botcherby for her insights on The Imposter Syndrome; Alexandra Jones who advised me on nutrition; Dr. Paul Hyman who ensured I was well fed; Dr. Kim Jobst whose insights into the meaning of disease have supported my work; Denise O'Dwyer whose homeopathic remedies kept me ticking; Ana Capone whose Opening the Heart helped me through much grief; Alexandra Watson whose coaching drew out my programme on Feminine Addictions; the late Professor Rolando Toro, creator of the extraordinary and powerful Biodanza system; Phillippa Kennon whose Biodanza classes nourished me week by week; Mike (Niraj) Skillbeck, Director of the Dorset School of Biodanza who generously gave me permission to use his beautifully worded descriptions, which I have integrated into 'Feminine Addictions' and 'Dancing with the Dark Side;' Philippe Lenaif whose Yin workshops shifted understandings deep within my soul; Guy Barrington whose Rites of Spring plunged me into the healing depths of mother/daughter relationships; Dr. Joanna Martin, founder of One of Many Women™ community and The One Woman Conference™ for inviting me to co-create and co-present alongside her; Sylvia Baldock for her Talent Dynamics profile test; Claire Elizabeth Terry who together with her colleague Oleguer Sarsanedas bravely edited my book, urging me on every step of the way; Mindy Gibbins-Klein and her team at Panoma Press for keeping me on my toes. And to those others without whose support I would have floundered more, I thank you.

To all those wonderful people who believed in me enough to provide testimonials, and the people who have supported this work as it goes out into the world, particularly Isabel Allende, Gloria Steinem, Courtney A. Walsh and Dr. Sam Collins. Thank you.

But above all, deep gratitude and appreciation to all the women leaders, particularly those unsung heroines, who have gone before and paved the way. Without you we would not be here. I am in awe of all that you have contributed.

80% of profits from this book will be donated to charities, together with raising funds for the 5th Worldwide Conference for Women
www.5wcw.org

Remember Our Power! by Gloria Steinem

In a time - indeed, for nearly all the time that human beings have walked the earth - you and I would have been living very differently: in small bands, raising our children together as if each child were the future of all of us, and migrating with the sun and seasons.

There were no nations, no lines drawn in the sand. Instead, there were paths and watering places, with trade and cultures blossoming wherever these paths came together in a pattern that spread like lace over the continents.

This was far from a primitive way of life. Indeed, inner space was explored and understood by the many, just as outer space is now explored and understood by the few.

If you and I had lived on what is now called Australia, disputes over paths and watering places would have been settled by who could "sing" the land the best, who knew the cliff that looked like a lizard or the hill that crouched like an animal, and who knew the length of the song it took to get there.

If you and I had lived here on this continent (the US) that the ancients called Turtle Island, we would have had talking circles, so each person could speak and listen until consensus was reached.

Yes, there were male chiefs, but they were chosen and advised by female elders. Yes, there were hard decisions, but they were made with seven future generations in mind.

In all of this, the goal was balance: between females and males, between each person, and the community between nature and humans - if, indeed, those things were thought of separately at all. As the Cherokee wise woman Rayna Green says, "On this continent, feminism - which also means womanism, mujerista-ism - is memory."

In ancient Africa, from which all of us came, no one had the deeds to children - and certainly not to women. Each of us belonged to ourselves and also to the community. Women had two or three children two or three years apart, no more than their health and mobility would allow, because women knew the power of herbs and timing, as women still do among the Kwei or San, the few so-called Bush People who still live in the original way of the Kalahari.

The goal of ancient games was cooperation, not competition. The most respected art was healing, not wounding. Violence was present, but only in self-defence.

I say all this because these are the things that have been programmed into our cells - for millennia. These are the true things for which our cellular memory still longs. We cannot go backward, but we can go forward with our whole selves and our whole memory.

What we have been raised to think of as inevitable - division and hierarchy, monotheism and nation states - actually accounts for less than ten percent of human history.

Ancient places … say, the Nubian temples of the Nile … depict God as all living things. As the great Egyptologist Henry Breasted said, "Monotheism is but imperialism in religion." We see this now as each side acts in the name of a god who looks like their rulers, a god who pretends that life after death is more honorable than life itself.

We must keep resisting and creating our way out of the recent hierarchical past in any way we can, but we will be stronger if each of us begins with our own bodies. They were not born to hurt or be hurt, and we can pledge never to use our bodies - or allow them to be used - in that way.

We will be stronger if we remember our own power.

We will all be stronger if we remember: there was another way. There is another way.

Reprinted by Kind Permission of Gloria Steinem and originally published in Ms. Magazine, Summer, 2003. Copyright © www.gloriasteinem.com

Foreword

A close look at the waves of feminism through history reveals feminist predecessors were women who refused to be adaptive to the status quo. They were marked by trailblazing, taking on challenges and aspiring to brighter horizons.

While women have been working towards this moment, we haven't been in the workforce all that long: women's suffrage began before the turn of the 20th century and had won the vote in the US by 1920 and in Britain by 1928; then those resilient 'Rosies' took over traditionally male jobs to support the war effort and most later withdrew to raise families in an unprecedented post-war economic expansion; then the bra-burning 60s and Equal Rights Amendment 70s that gave way to women entering the workforce en masse in the 80s and 90s.

Once accepted into the corporate world, many of us 'leaned in' and suppressed our femininity, worked like men and avoided discussions of an outside life or motherhood for fear of losing our credibility. Others tried relishing the victory only to discover the very environment devalued the feminine as soft; finding ourselves dominated, not necessarily by men, but by the distorted concept of masculinity pervasive in big business. Many women started their own businesses or opted to remain at home, but for many neither option really suited - a quiet and resentful generation of women has been brewing without rocking the boat too much.

And over two decades later where do we stand? The Global Gender Gap Report ranks Britain 26th, its lowest overall score for equality since 2008; with the US not much further ahead at 20th... Where is the gender leadership from these so-called leaders of the free world?

Yet there is a new wave building momentum, not far off shore. And it's a tsunami with enough potential energy to sweep away these archaic masculine-dominated forms of business once for all... and for one simple reason: If business can't embrace the new feminine, they stand to lose more than half their talent – and what's more, they won't be able to fill those vacancies with qualified men because, surprise, many new generation men want to see the same changes!

15

What we are seeing now is a new growing solidarity among women. And from a historical perspective, it's about time for the next feminist wave to break. This new generation of women of all ages, all backgrounds, stands ready to fully embrace their feminine strengths, identify with them and change the world with them; simultaneously refusing to identify with traditional feminism as a concept, and instead fully experience the power of their gender in collaboration with their masculine counterparts in the workforce and the world.

Let's not 'man up' or change who we are – we must redefine the systems and structures so that they work for women, unashamed to put family first, having pride in what makes us different. More women leaders must rise to the top ranks of business, politics and community power to provide new perspectives and new leadership for the world's pressing issues, which are legion.

The world needs our help desperately, threatened on all sides from issues economic, environmental, geopolitical, societal and technological. The World Economic Forum's latest report calls these "global risks of highest concern." Who better qualified to help take a refreshingly new approach to these issues than women with our unique perspective as mothers, sisters, and daughters?

As women, we must learn to rely on our intuition, gut feelings and instincts, which society either minimises or rationalises away. And rather than ask women to conform to masculine-patterned styles of leadership, as is commonly found in the business world, we must challenge others to realise these valuable feminine qualities are indispensible to the businesses in which we work and not least of all, to the world at large.

At a time when women are increasingly dissatisfied with our work lives and desire for balance, combined with the world suffering from some of the most dramatic issues in our history, we need to send out a clear message: women can change the world, if we join together, focus on our strengths and rely on our inner strength, instead of blindly accepting a path that we have been told by society is the only route to success.

I applaud Susie Heath's contribution to helping us make this vital change.

Dr Sam Collins, Founder and CEO, Aspire Trailblazing Women
www.aspirewomen.com Author of 'Radio Heaven.'

Contents

Introduction

The 21st Century is proving to be momentous for women. We're now coming to the fore, stepping into roles as major breadwinners, high achievers and creators of new wealth. In fact, as I write, the number of women in UK boardrooms is rising significantly. In several countries in Europe, women are now entering ministerial roles in areas such as Defence, and making strong headway in the worlds of science, television and filmmaking and even in that old male bastion, the Church. Women are being sworn in as Government ministers in Italy and Spain for their competence rather than to fulfil political guidelines. In England, over 70% of new businesses are being created by women, over 50% of high street shops are now being opened and run by women, and women also account for 85% of all buying decisions. We've also excelled in the Olympic Games, particularly in some sports which were traditionally the domain of men, while women have led much of the commentary.

This pattern of women stepping up into strong leadership roles in so many areas is being echoed all over the Western world.

However, along with leadership comes the ever-present threat of burnout, as success for some comes at too high a price. Many women are falling by the wayside because their aims and expectations are still based on the masculine paradigm set by captains of industry as far back as the Industrial Revolution. They've been taught to lead in a masculine way, emulating men in all that they do. And many find themselves failing miserably, for the simple reason that being a second-rate man rather than a first-rate woman is inauthentic, exhausting and demoralising. They end up being what I call, 'Men in Frocks'.

As a result, we're seeing many women leave their high-powered positions in the corporate market to create their own successful home-based businesses. If this is you, I applaud you – we need women like you, because I believe that entrepreneurs are the future of humanity. They're driving human progress, creating jobs and building real value in the world. But we need to be able to retain women in positions of high status in corporations too.

My intention in this book is to introduce you to a new model of leadership, to help ensure that you don't burn out, that you stay on top of the game, and to give you some tools and strategies to help you succeed in whichever arena you choose.

I encourage you to let go of the addiction to old behaviours which have been holding you back, to stop following the herd, to step into your own leadership, both at a personal and professional level, and to encourage you to facilitate change – change that will leave a legacy for future generations.

If you're not formally in a leadership role, you may not think of yourself as expressing leadership. But in today's world, each of us is being called upon to express our own unique leadership. My belief is that it's not large corporations who will shape the future, but women like you and me stepping in and claiming our leadership as women.

No matter what you do, whether you're a CEO, a nurse, a scientist, a mother, a teacher, a politician, an entrepreneur, a pilot, an actor, a musician, a chef – you name it! – *you* express leadership through *your* unique perspective.

I call on you as a woman to tap into the potency of your feminine awareness, knowledge and authenticity, and to bring a new dimension into leadership around the world.

Because NOW *is* our time!

Chapter 1
The World Needs You!

We're living in a time of chaos and change, with systems breaking down all around us. Day by day, we're faced with events that shock us to the core as institutions we've relied on collapse, and leaders and people we've trusted are brought to justice for corruption and crimes against society. The planet is changing at an unprecedented pace, with new technology and systems forcing us to adapt faster than ever before, making life more complex, ambiguous and challenging. So, it's all the more important that we have leaders we can look up to, aspire to, and above all, trust.

We generally think we understand Leadership. But historically, this has been mainly from a male perspective, which is no longer viable in these times of planetary transformation.

Much of my training was based on a very masculine paradigm. It taught me wonderful strategies to survive in a male-dominated world, but in time, it caused me to question not only who I was, but what it was doing to me as a woman. Over the years, many books have been published on the subject of leadership where softer skills have been introduced, but so much is changing now that we need a new paradigm to uncover what authentic leadership is really about in the 21st century.

I believe that we need truly conscious, authentic leaders who are adaptable, resourceful, trustworthy, caring, self-reliant, productive and ethical, and who contribute to the wellbeing of the planet as a whole.

Like most inventors of the past, who've contributed to so many extraordinary creations, leaders will need to access sources of information that are intuitive and non-rational, and make a stand for what they believe in. They will also need to have greater awareness, understand how organizations can be a force for change, and be able to navigate their way through this complex interrelated world. Recently, several major companies have stopped recruiting people for their educational qualifications alone, and are now actively seeking out those who are intuitive.

Cue the women!

So, does this imply that we have no further use for men? Not in the slightest. Masculine and feminine dynamics reside within both genders, as well as in the external areas of our lives. Feminine Leadership needs to live alongside Masculine Leadership, to co-exist as collaborators and co-creators. There are aspects within men that we as women need desperately; there are aspects within women that men need desperately. We need to show them a new way of living and of being in the world, and to lead them by the hand, so that they can live in their empowered masculine to help co-create a magnificent world.

The Dalai Lama himself said:

"The future of the planet lies in the hands of the Western Woman."

I feel now that as technology has opened up our world, women leaders in developing countries are also stepping up and owning their power. The future is bright and the future is female!

You can't ignore this call any more – it's echoing across the planet.

Are you the best leader you can be?
If not, why not?
What's stopping you?

The leadership establishment is equated with inflexibility or, in many cases, immobility. We desperately need leaders – especially women – who can offer flexibility of thought, facilitate creative new solutions in a fast-changing world, rally resources and think in new ways.

I use the word 'dance' as a perfect metaphor for this navigation, this ability to change and adapt, to flow, to co-operate with others, to give and receive feedback, to listen intently, to embrace diversity, to work with perfect timing and to express yourself with every pore of your being.

Leaders are renowned for having Presence, a quality that, like a magnet, draws to itself resources, favourable circumstances, helpful people and commitment. I'm not talking about personality traits here: it's about your state of being, the way you show up in the world, a state that you can generate yourself. This book teaches you how.

Within our perpetually shifting environment, you need to be in a state of present-time awareness, dancing with the moment of whatever shows up, with people, with ideas, with circumstances, with attitudes, with unexpected situations, and to be able to handle it all with equanimity. So as not to get dragged down into circumstances, yet remaining fully aware of them. So as to maintain your clarity, your purpose and your freedom to respond with the right decisions during a crisis, without getting swept up into the drama of the situation. So as to have a clear perspective on things and remain open to all possibilities.

In my years of coaching and training, I've heard many women talk about their lack of confidence, or how their self-esteem has taken a knock, how much they self-sabotage, how tired they feel or how much they fear being found out – the 'Imposter Syndrome'. If any of these resonate with you, or if you've had even a whisper of burnout, I urge you to join me on the journey here. If you're exhausted with 'Fake it till you make it', or can't get your head around some of the constant striving and demands of modern work life, or if the work/life balance eludes you, then this is the book for you!

I've felt pregnant with this book for a long time now, as it has almost 'demanded' to be written. It's not the usual type of leadership book: it doesn't present facts and figures about boardrooms and internal politics. It doesn't tell you how many women have been elevated to CEO status, advise you on the structure for leadership in the corporate market, or how to deal with your boss.

It's not full of pie charts or profiling tests or lists of statistics or references to tomes that you are never going to look up for yourself. In fact, when I tried to write it from a more intellectual perspective, my external hard drive with all my back-ups mysteriously crashed, and I lost weeks of dedicated writing, along with all my research, which I thought had been safely preserved. So I had a choice: to begin the research all over again and rewrite without many of the statistics and papers I had so carefully pored through, or to just let it come from my core, my guts and my heart, to be open, vulnerable and as authentic as I possibly could be. And this is what I did.

It feels somewhat risky, but if I don't stick my head above the parapet, I won't be able to help the thousands of women who appear serene on the outside, yet deep under the water are frantically paddling like crazy to keep afloat.

What *Dance Your Way To The Top!* does is to take you deep inside yourself to awaken your passionate longing for a different world; your true desire to bring who you really are, with all your unique skills and innate talents to the table; to become the leader of your own life first, before you lead others. And to do it now! No one is more qualified to transform your life than you are, hence Dance *Your* Way!

This book teaches you a new way of leadership and of getting to the top, not by clinging to the ladder with immaculately painted fingernails, only to realise when you get there that not only may the ladder be leaning against the wrong wall, but that there's a fire blazing at the top! It teaches you instead to dance with authority, to dance with adversity and to dance with passion, resilience, creativity and your personal life force, in both a metaphorical and a literal sense, and to do so in conjunction with your health, vitality and wellbeing.

Dance Your Way To The Top! gives you permission to come off your perpetual treadmill of thoughts and automatic ways of doing things, and to connect instead with the innate wisdom of your own body.

It invites you to uncover and reveal the authentic you, to dance bravely out into the world and to give yourself permission to be fully self-expressed in whatever you choose to do. It teaches you those things that you already know, deep inside, but haven't yet dared to admit out loud. *Dance Your Way To The Top!* is about healthy, warm-hearted, life-enhancing leadership. Please don't underestimate the power of some of the material in this book; I have witnessed it change individuals, companies and even the government of a small country.

The methodology in this book embraces a combination of new mind-technology, physiology and connection to that deeper part of you which 'knows'. This is the opportunity for you to *experience* in every cell of your body what success is like: what relaxation, joy, creativity, wildness, passion, fluidity, resilience, success and vitality actually *feel* like, rather than just pushing and urging yourself on from the confines of your thoughts and your past experiences, which can limit you dramatically.

This book won't suit everyone. If you have a particularly rational, logical mind, you may find it doesn't appeal because many of the exercises require that you use your physicality, that you move your body accompanied by selected music. But before you rush to toss it away, I'd like to suggest to you that when you plumb its depths, you may discover a part of you that you buried a long time ago, which is crying out for expression. And that, if you give yourself permission, you'll change and grow beyond your wildest imaginings – from *Becoming* a leader into *Being* a leader.

As Einstein said:

"Any intelligent fool can make things bigger, more complex, and more violent. It takes a touch of genius - and a lot of courage - to move in the opposite direction."

Through the exercises here, you'll experience moments that shift your perception. You'll tap into elements that leave you feeling more true to yourself, more creative, happy, fulfilled, energised, and connected with your feminine strength and potency in a way you may never have dared before.

Dance Your Way To The Top! flies in the face of traditional strategies and structures, and takes you to a place where to lead is to lead from the feminine. It will beguile you, charm you, annoy you, frustrate, excite and seduce you. And then, like opening a door, release you from all those imprisoning thoughts and behaviours that have held you back, to reveal the magnificence of who you really are. It will enable you to move through the world with your potential unleashed, with compassion for yourself, alongside empathy and consideration for others, and with a deep knowing of your unique contribution to making this world a better place. This is about being the difference that makes the difference!

This is an invitation to join me, and millions of other women around the world, in being agents of transformation, and so leave a legacy on this beautiful planet that we have the privilege of calling 'Home' for a fleeting span of time.

Let the dance begin!

Chapter 2
A Letter to the Men

Gentlemen,

If you happen to see this book lying around, please don't jump to conclusions and think that women are trying to usurp your place and take over the world, or that the women in your life are plotting behind your back!

In fact, what I hope you will realise as you read this special letter to you is that this book is not about the rise of women at the expense of men. Rather, the feminine is rising up to meet you, so *together* we can create a planet where we all want to live.

This is an opportunity for both sexes to have better relationships, more profitable businesses and a better world!

Archbishop Desmond Tutu is quoted as saying if he had one wish to change the world, he would have more women leaders. At Davos, joking that he may need security to escort him offstage, he suggested:

"What we need is a revolution by women. I think women ought to be saying to us men: 'You have made a mess. Just get out and let us in!'"

I'm in awe of all that man has created. When I Googled 'Innovations by Men', I came up with an amazing list of 50 things without which we wouldn't have the extraordinary benefits most of us take for granted these days. Without some of them, I wouldn't be able to write this book, nor you read it! In fact I doubt any of us would be alive today without these incredible inventions, and for those I am truly grateful. What brilliant minds, what talent and what genius.

However, I'm angry. In fact, I'm very angry, and if you've ever been on the wrong end of a woman's wrath, then you will be afraid – very afraid!

Anger for a woman often remains as pent-up energy, and many times turns in on itself to manifest as deep sadness, anxiety, depression and hurt. But what lies beneath is pure unadulterated anger which remains unexpressed, and eats away at our organs, our sensuality, our authenticity, our deep relationships with you – our men – our beauty and our joy, as we try to hold it all in for fear of being judged, and because we've been taught to be 'good girls'.

However, when we have the space to unleash our anger and allow it to flow through our bodies, and to process it through hearing our emotions fully expressed in our own words, a whole new feisty, juicy energy arises which I happen to know that you guys really respond to and admire.

It's when we get shut down that we become unresourceful, disconnected from our sexual energy, resentful and whiny.

So rather than run away or stick your fingers in your ears, or judge, or try and solve the issue in our stead, please hold on for a moment! When a woman has the courage to be really angry and express how she feels, it's worth your while listening to her – and I mean *really* listening, not just with your ears, but with your gut, your heart and your soul too – because what she says may well change your perceptions, leading to a life of deeper fulfilment, understanding, satisfaction, closeness and joy. I invite you to be curious here, as curiosity is one of the most important things you own.

When we look back in history, many great men used to seek counsel from the woman in their life before making major decisions, so please listen up! Once my rant is over, I will return to my calm loving self again, but what has to be said here is vital, and *must* out.

You see, last year I was watching television (a rare event), but the programme that had me glued to my sofa was a trip around the globe in ninety minutes from a scientist's eye view from 220 miles up in space on the International Space Station, *Shuttle Atlantis,* on its final voyage, orbiting Planet Earth.

This spectacular TV programme documented what was happening to another amazing spaceship, the one on which we are all hurtling through space – what the presenter called: "This small jewelled ball of rock we call Planet Earth, a world on which we all depend."

While I was settling down in my innocence to watch the wonders of the world, the natural beauty, the magnificence of forests and rivers, plant and animal life, what I saw instead was much of the damage we've inflicted on it over the last few decades which include:

- The scars on the lungs of the world, 447 acres of our miraculous Amazon rainforest lost every 90 minutes, along with all its healing plants and medicines;

- The devastating effects of plastics which don't decompose; 40,000 tonnes of plastic produced worldwide every 90 minutes, the majority of which will be thrown away;

- The Aral Sea in Kazakhstan which has been bled dry and now sits arid, filled with chemicals;

- The orange–yellow pall of fog sitting over the industrialised country of China;

- The chilling statistic that governments around the world spend $257m on weapons and war, every 90 minutes;

- The fact that Ethiopia, the cradle of civilisation, has become so overpopulated that 23,019 children are born every 90 minutes.

I was so horrified and distressed by what I saw, that suddenly like a volcano, all this anger and outrage started bubbling up inside me and I realised that if I shoved it down, or went into sweet peaceful mode as a way of distracting myself, it would become detrimental (as do all negative emotions) to my body and to those around me. I know too, that as you're reading this, you also will have feelings of fear, anger and upset moving around your body as you read the above list.

The world I know and love is teetering on the edge of destruction and annihilation as we move towards an untenable 9 billion population by 2050.

So I took pen to paper and allowed the anger to come out. This is what poured off my pen:

- I'm angry that my beloved grandfather was shot in the head in the trenches during the senseless First World War and had to live with blinding headaches and tortuous memories all his life as a result.

- I'm angry that bombs are being dropped in so many places around this fragile planet with no thought to the consequences of the impact on the landmasses, and the possibility that, like the theory of the butterfly wing, this may result in land-shifts and Tsunamis.

- I'm angry that terrorism is so rife that we live under the perpetual threat of war; that skirmishes are breaking out all over the world accompanied by so much violence and hatred.

- I'm angry that the banks have caused such mayhem and that our financial 'recession' and scaremongering has caused so many problems for us.

- I'm angry that seven of my beautiful women friends have died of breast cancer and that every one of them had parabens in her body through chemicals found in beauty and household products.

- I'm angry about the floating island of plastic waste that never breaks down properly, which threatens our oceans and islands. And how the plastics affect hormones in creatures in the food chain and in our own beautiful bodies as well.

- I'm angry that I had to nurse my beloved father and mother through their deaths of cancer over the last couple of years, when there are many known cures that cost virtually nothing, but yet the pharmaceutical companies insist on denying their existence.

- I'm angry that there's enough money in the world for every man, woman and child to have $1 million each, yet two-thirds of the world lives in poverty.

- I'm angry that the elderly, with their wisdom of the ages, are treated with disrespect in my home country (the UK).

- I'm angry that there is so much light pollution that the birds and animals don't know whether it's day or night.

- I'm angry that technology has robbed us of good, warm-hearted connection and communication and a close community, resulting in terrible loneliness for many.

- I'm angry that our homes and offices are built with products and chemicals which make us sick.

- I'm angry that our food is slowly poisoning us, that instead of (for the most part) natural organically grown fresh produce, we're consuming indistinguishable packages of food, full of additives and chemicals and genetically modified substances which taste completely different from the real thing, and that we're being lured and seduced into destroying our health.

- I'm angry that out of the top DVDs and computer games sold in the shops, many of them contain violence, cruelty or aggressive sexual scenes. Even those aimed at five-year-old boys seem to be full of punching and kicking, bombs and annihilation, which even if they are cartoon characters, seep into the unconscious.

- I'm angry that some of our most precious animals are being hunted to the point of extinction.

- I'm angry that animal husbandry is still very cruel in many parts of the world.

- I'm angry about the mountain of wasted food that gets thrown away at the end of every day in supermarkets because of rules and regulations and 'health and safety'. All that food could be given to the homeless or nursing homes or poorer families.

- I'm angry at the way women are portrayed in the media, that we're made to feel inadequate because of our breasts or our bottoms or our cellulite or our wrinkles.

- I'm angry about discrimination, particularly against women, age and race.

- I'm angry to see the number of women who get burned-out in business, because they're being lured into behaving like men, with the resultant damage to their health, their hormones, their fertility and their wellbeing.

- I'm angry that women are not respected the way they should be in business – that some men still think it's OK to behave in a macho, sexist and emotionally abusive manner towards women.

- I'm angry that when I buy something cheap from China or India, I'm adding to sweatshop labour – but if I don't buy, they'll starve anyway. I'm put in such a moral dilemma.

- I'm angry that women continue to be raped and tortured and treated like second-class citizens in many parts of the world.

- I'm angry that some men in business take their clients to strip clubs and call it 'client entertainment', and that women's jobs are threatened if they don't agree to go along too.

- I'm angry that the porn industry is teaching boys as young as ten that women should be shaved and bare like prepubescent teenagers and that sex is just a commodity.

- I'm angry that 20% of the female workforce in the UK has to take time off work due to violence in the home.

- I'm angry that young women are being groomed to satisfy the sick appetite of some men, and that trafficking is seen as acceptable to so many.

- I'm angry that pedophiles are so prevalent and are stealing away the innocence of our young people.

- I'm angry that at least 120 million girls and women have experienced female genital mutilation in the 29 countries in Africa and the Middle East where the practice is concentrated. Given present trends, as many as 30 million girls under the age of 15 may still be at risk. Female genital mutilation is demanded by many men, and carried out by women. The effects on these women and young girls are devastating.

I'm not alone in my anger: when I put a survey out on Facebook recently asking women what made them angry, what came up was war, injustice, poverty, violation of human rights, human trafficking, grooming young girls for prostitution, inhuman treatment of animals, destroying the creation of this amazing planet... the list went on.

I can't get my head around why this is all still happening in the second decade of the 21st century. It just doesn't make sense in this day and age, when more and more people are becoming aware of what's happening around them.

When I look over the list above (and it's certainly not all that troubles me), the simple fact is that most of it is not perpetrated by women. We have not had a say in much of it, as during the last umpteen years of patriarchal society, we've been dictated to and sold up the ole Swannee River by men.

How many women do you know who drop bombs or cut down the rainforest? How many women do you know who perpetrate war, or demand that we fill our bodies with chemicals that kill us, or genetically engineer crops that will make us ill, or abuse other women? How many women do you know who prey on small children and sexually molest them?

It's time to say STOP! Stop the aggressive, destructive, manipulative masculine energy that causes so much pain and devastation. Let us have a new, more loving and more generative way of living in this world.

And this can only happen if women are given a greater say in leadership.

Now, before you think I'm some raving angry feminist and anti-men, let me tell you I adore most of the men I know. My grandfather was a wonderful soul; my father was a leading light in my life and gave me opportunities to meet some extraordinary people. I am the mother of a daughter and two sons, all of whom I'm very proud, grandmother to two little fellas, and sister to a brilliant businessman. I have been girlfriend and wife, lover and beloved, and also have a host of men friends whom I adore and who in turn, adore and cherish me.

As I was writing this chapter, my second little grandson was born, and I want him to be able to breathe clean air, walk in beautiful forests and revel in the joys of nature when he grows up.

This anger isn't sexist, or one of war or retaliation or hatred or justification. It is one of pure outrage that the precious planet I live on is being exploited; that so much of everything we've based our existence on is falling apart, and will continue to do so, unless there is *radical change*.

I am asking the women of the world to feel outrage: to be outrageous, to come out of their sense of powerlessness and subordination, and to use their outrage as a springboard for change. You can't change the world from a place of anger – it's a state of powerlessness and non-rationality which can cause even greater damage, as we've seen from all the wars, but at least it has passion in it. However, passion can tie us up into a place of desperation, so we need to transmute it to a passionate heart – and a passionate heart can do much good.

As Gandhi said to his grandson:

"We all feel anger. Anger can strike like lightning and
split a living tree. Or it can be channeled, transformed.
A switch can be flipped and it can shed light like a lamp."

Women are wired to be more heart-centred, while men are wired to be more mind-centred, which is why we can work so well together as a team. The heart is 5,000 times more intelligent than the brain – our minds only know what has been before, and is based on many years of conditioning. So, to make decisions from our minds only is not where true intelligence lies. We have to use both our minds and our hearts.

Women have a deep understanding and concern for the future – we have the ability to reach into the future and have a 'knowing' about the consequences of what's happening in the present. You men are very much more present-time aware. It's the nature and wiring of our different brains. We are still wired-up as cave men and cave women, and little has changed over the centuries. But without each other, we won't survive. It takes millions of sperm fighting to reach one egg, to create life. Life doesn't happen on its own – it's a co-creative project.

Consciousness, however, is changing on the planet. Both corporations and individuals are being 'outed' for not being authentic. Governments have been toppled and exposed for not saying what's truly going on.

In this technological age where transparency is paramount, we are all being called upon to be authentic and congruent: because if not, we're just covering up, faking it and losing the trust of those around us in the process.

As women, we've got it wrong in the past – we thought we had to be like you and then wanted you to be like us. As a result, we've emasculated you and masculinised ourselves, failing to honour the differences between us. We've been afraid to speak up, to speak our truth, to express our true feelings about this. We've been told that to reach the top in any corporation, we have to let go of what it feels like to be a natural woman – that we need to warp and change ourselves beyond recognition so that we become more and more like the men we wish to emulate. And we've done it – some of us have got there. But at what price? The world isn't any safer; we still lie in our beds worrying. In fact, it seems that what used to be the number one killer – stress, which accounts for a massive 78% of doctors' visits, is now morphing into anxiety, a different state altogether.

It's time for feminine wisdom to step forward, or quite simply, we won't have a world worth living in or saving. Yes, we still have a lot to learn, to remember, to assimilate. You men teach us about death – we women are here to teach you about life and joy and beauty and wildness and authenticity and cooperation and tenderness and nurturing and intimacy at the deepest level.

I know you may be saying that you're in touch with your wonderful feminine qualities, and yes, the feminine needs to be resurrected within men as well as within women. But we also need you men to reclaim your authentic, powerful, protective masculine, so we can work in co-operation with each other, rather than competition.

As women we've fought to ensure that we can do anything just as well as, if not better than men, but, apart from childbirth, our bodies are not built with the same strength and endurance, without putting our health and our hormones at risk. I know some women are going to challenge me here, but how much better off would it be if we asked you guys to step up and do the protecting and all the things which are not within our natural disposition? Women aren't particularly good at asking for help – we feel it makes us look weak after all we've struggled for, but we're not asking you to step down – we're asking you to step up, help stop the madness, say "No!" to much of what's happening in the world, be a force for good and spread the word, and support women.

Encourage other men to be honourable and act with integrity to bring your strong masculine energy, together with our potent, generous and compassionate feminine energy, to generate something the world has never seen before.

And you as real men are the ones to do it!

As a male friend of mine, scientist and coach Jazz Rasool says:

"I realised men had had their day, with their visions and their women supporting them, and now it was time for women to actualise their visions and for the men to provide the technical support and logistics to manifest women's plans for peace and an elimination of war."

So my invitation to you is to find a woman with a vision, a dream, and help her bring it into reality with your ability to push through, using your systems, your logic and your analytical brains. Not to take over, not to make it yours, but to support her in her highest truth and to bring the beauty back onto this earth.

Could she do it herself? Quite probably – but would she want to? The cost to her health, her vibrancy and her juicy energy would be too much. Many of the most successful businesses I know who are contributing to the world today are a collaboration of male and female energies, a synchronous dance in pairs, and they work, they really work! When we collaborate on these issues, a new world will emerge, one in which you are proud and overjoyed to live. Your contribution matters. Your cooperation matters. Your collaboration matters.

Thank you gentlemen, for reading this.

I look forward to meeting you some day out there in a world where peace and creativity co-exist.

Chapter 3
Why Feminine Leadership?

Do you ever have days where you feel stressed at work, anxious and frustrated, under pressure to succeed, overwhelmed, exhausted, powerless to make any real and lasting difference and maybe even a little depressed?

Do you occasionally find yourself saying: "There has to be a better way?"

Yet do you also feel a sense of urgency, a stirring deep within you that you can't quite articulate, a sense that something momentous is about to happen in the world?

If that's so, you are not alone. We live in incredibly exciting times, arguably the best time ever to be alive. However, there is also a strong sense that we're at a critical turning point in history, when so much of what we've known and relied upon is being thrown into disarray.

There is an urgency and profound concern as we face social, political, financial and environmental changes which, if not addressed, will throw the whole world into even greater chaos.

And time is running out.
If we don't do something quickly, the world which we know
and love will change beyond recognition.

No matter our race or religion, our sexual orientation, our colour or creed – we are all facing the same potential disasters on the planet: overcrowding, insufficient resources, lack of education, global warming, environmental destruction – and so much more.

Technology is changing at such a high rate of knots that the moment a new gadget is launched in the marketplace, it's already out of date as something even more revolutionary is being developed. Communication is almost instantaneous with events happening on the world stage being transmitted to our awareness within milliseconds.

Knowledge and information is at our fingertips – literally. What was once available to the select few is now available for millions upon millions of people around the world. In fact, we're exposed to more information in just one day than our great-grandparents were in a lifetime. Is it any wonder that we're overwhelmed?

Humanity is at a crisis point. While it's not feasible to turn the clock back, it's worth having a brief glimpse at how history has evolved to its present way of life. Archaeological sites excavated in Old Europe from 7,000 years ago to 3,500 BCE show that mankind and womankind lived harmoniously in locations chosen for their beautiful settings, where water ran freely and pastures were abundant for growing crops and raising animals. There was stability as these societies developed pottery and artefacts from copper, as well as jewellery. A rudimentary script was formed; there was trade, sailing and communication, and women took charge of the wealth while the men were the protectors.

The whole concept of woman as the provider of life was honoured, and the goddess was worshipped as a symbol of fertility and bounty. This was not a matriarchal society but one where neither gender was subordinate to the other. Here too, there was no evidence of warfare.

Once it was discovered that men had a part to play in fertility, the powerful, strong masculine took control. These heroes of old became masters of the wild as they conquered land, climbed mountains, forded rivers and took to the seas.

Over time, warrior people from the north swept through the land, dominating the goddess culture and incorporating it into their ways. Physical strength, weapons and military strategy thus became dominant as the old ways of honouring the feminine fell by the wayside.

Once the alphabet became widespread, the written and spoken word began to hold authority socially, politically and within religious circles. The rest, as they say, is *his*-story.

However, the men who have shaped our world have failed to make this planet a safe place in which to experience the fullness of our lives. And so, now, we as women and mothers of men are being called to do something about it. We have been under patriarchal rule for over 4,000 years – a structure that enforces and expresses authority and power – but which is outmoded, out-of-date and no longer applicable as we move through the 21st century.

It's now time to disentangle masculinity from the stereotypical association it has come to represent, with its domination, control and violence in so many areas of society, and to introduce a sustainable balance and harmony through what I call the 'potency' of feminine energy. Which is where you come in! We can no longer afford to sit on the sidelines and wait for other people to deal with the problems.

Male leadership cannot possibly change the fundamentals of this masculine hierarchy that has ruled for so long. For there to be a harmonious world where those who are living without power *matter*, strong feminine women like you need to speak up for the children, women, animals, the environment, and for our beautiful planet itself.

We need women's wisdom, women's experience, women's compassion and women's common sense in those areas where decisions are taken that affect all of our lives.

We're living in a time of unprecedented change in human history – never before has there been so much rapid change, and never before has there been so much potentiality for women.

In fact, we are on the brink of an evolutionary shift, with the potential to alter the course of history. We as women, have the opportunity to stop the present madness and make the difference that is so needed right now, have a powerful input and make an impact on shaping the course of our future.

But not in the way we've been doing up till now: trying to fight male energy with our own version of the same, as if we were ashamed of being female. It doesn't work – not for us, nor society, nor business, our relationships, our children, and certainly not for the planet.

In recent years, there's been a huge loss of a sense of direction in the female world, as we've succumbed to the pressures of glossy magazines and the latest fad diet, to plastic surgery and to changing the way we look by external means, along with a major misunderstanding of a woman's role on the earth.

Millions of women around the world, whether in business for ourselves or working in larger corporations, as mothers or teachers or artists, are now feeling a call to reclaim the potency of the feminine aspect of our nature. This feeling of being 'on the edge' is in response to the mammoth change that's happening worldwide as we're being called to bring forth a new dawn to this planet and humanity, to birth it into a new era.

I believe that Western women in particular are ALL being called to leadership at this pivotal point in history, because we have the privilege of a good education, of enough money to feed and clothe ourselves and also the technology to be able to put into practice the methods which I'll be talking about here. And as other developing nations join with us, bringing their wisdom, experience, knowledge and understanding, together we will be able to create the world we all dream of.

Some highly successful businesswomen are relinquishing their jobs and choosing instead to become full-time mothers; others are letting go of their high-pressured jobs to immerse themselves in what they truly love – in what makes their heart sing.

Others still are delving deeper into their own personal and spiritual development, while some are devoting more time to contribute to society through healing or working with charities; some are stepping into leadership roles to be change-makers, following their passionate desire for a shift in society.

Whatever is happening, many are feeling an urgent need for love and intimacy, a deeper connection with their loved ones and a true desire to live in a more fulfilling way than the shallowness of societal conditioning. Some may feel a deep 'knowing' (and this may be you) that you have a unique purpose in the world, and long to fulfil that purpose.

As I said before, no matter what your role, whether you're a film star, a princess, a singer, a bank manager, an entrepreneur or even a 'lady of the night', we are all being encouraged to step into leadership, right here and right now.

Why do I think this? Because the world is at a tipping point – we've been surrounded by so much chaos and uncertainty over the last five years as the pillars of society have crumbled around our ears. Several corporations and much of our banking system have fallen, and our health system is teetering on the edge.

There is an Undernet we didn't know existed in our own sweet innocence, which is robbing our children of their youth. Technology is soaring off into the stratosphere, and most of us have very little idea as to where it might lead in the future.

Is this what you want for your planet? Is this what you want for your grandchildren, to have so very little oxygen left for them to breathe, for there to be a scarcity of real food, for humanity to be dulled down as we give more and more of our power away to industry and technology? Isn't it time to say STOP?

We've come a long way since our forebears chained themselves to the railings so that we could cast our vote, and since we had to use camel dung, crocodile spittle and sheep's intestines to control our fertility. We have access to more money, opportunity, education and freedom than any other generation in history. But has it made us more fulfilled? Deep down, many of us feel we haven't yet attained the things that are dearest to our hearts – including a safe world for our children and the future generations to come.

It's this deep ache in the heart that I want to address in this book.

It isn't government and big businesses and major religions that will change the fate of our planet. It is you and me, the way we think, the way we behave and what we create in our lives, individually and collectively, that will influence everything in the world. By leading ourselves first, we influence everything and everyone around us, and I believe we have a responsibility to do so.

I know I'm going to press a few buttons here, but we have to get rid of the idea of 'Empowering Women'. That's male energy. 'Assertiveness for women' – also male energy! 'Pushing through the glass ceiling'… male energy yet again.

Power means 'power over' and that's not where the strength of the feminine lies. To seek power over the other doesn't nourish the soul.

It's time to get away from being disappointed, angry, raging feminists because that too is just more distorted male energy. It's now time to change and own our own unique 'softer feminine power'.

The male arena is difficult enough for men to operate in, particularly where the challenges tend to be more cerebral rather than physical, but even harder for us as women. When you look around and see women behaving aggressively or being very masculine, they have effectively 'borrowed' masculine energy, copying the strategies which men use, but the results in our bodies can be devastating as we're utilising energy which doesn't come to us naturally. It's actually our emergency energy which, when we use too much of it, burns us out.

Many women have learned to operate using too much of this Yang or masculine energy, but it leaves us feeling shallow, empty and unfulfilled, as we operate out of the insecurity of being a woman, and with a lack of understanding of our own intrinsic femininity.

We've achieved so much from the equality we've been demanding, working successfully in what were once male-dominated professions, trying to beat them at their own game, but the consequences are literally killing us, as we take our lives further away from the equilibrium we were initially seeking.

If what we were doing as women were really working, there would be peace among nations, an end to environmental disasters and poverty and many of our social issues would be resolved.

Mother Earth herself is ailing! As humans, we're arrogant enough to believe that we have to save the planet, but she has her own systems of change and regulation and regeneration in the form of earthquakes and volcanoes, floods and tsunamis, droughts and hurricanes. So she will go on in some shape or form even if we have polluted her beauty through our toxic fumes, our chemical waste and our destructive bombs.

It's the human race and nature's bountiful birds, animals and plants that are endangered. No other planet can sustain life the way Earth does – there isn't a spare Earth when we run out of resources here! This is now or never time – we can't wait for future generations, because at the rate we're going, there will be none!

Earth is the only source of life and we must nurture it at any cost.

Chapter 4
The New Feminine Paradigm

Never before have we, as women, held in our own hands so many infinite possibilities for shaping the future of our world and human civilisation.

Einstein noted that we can't solve a problem from the level at which it was created, and thus we need a new level of awareness, a new way of thinking, a new way of behaving, a new way of relating, a new way of leading, so that our species can evolve together as nature intended.

Women I coach talk about constant hyper-vigilance, of being unable to switch off at night and tossing and turning in their beds, waking in the morning feeling ragged and wrung-out, and going through their day in a disempowered stupor.

Dumbing-down, covering-up or just not daring to get in touch with our feelings and emotions for fear of being judged, thought of as neurotic, or as having 'women's problems', or simply not being heard, we often hide behind what I call 'Feminine Addictions' which I'll cover later in this book.

And so, we women have shape-shifted and wriggled and forced our way into being accepted, into being one of the boys, all in the quest to fit in. Yet at what cost? Burnout, childlessness, lack of deep, meaningful relationships and intimacy, lack of authenticity, disappointment, lack of credibility, lack of self-esteem and deep, deep dissatisfaction. Even some of those who really have reached the top echelons have often done so at risk to their mental and physical health as we've subdued so many of those amazing qualities that make us quintessentially feminine in order to fit in with business. Business is a masculine paradigm and it's served us very well and, indeed, is invaluable to task-focused operations and activities, as seen in strong leaders with a steely determination to build business and profit. But now is the time for *feminine wisdom* to flow. Feminine energy in business is the glue that holds relationships together and is the key to cultural and environmental harmony.

Imagine what it will be like when we create a new operating model in business where women work to the best of their skills and talents, using nature's timing, in the areas where they're likely to be most creative and feel more fulfilled, as this is where true accomplishment and the best outcomes lie.

I'm asking you to find your authentic sweet spot, to come out of your logical, linear masculine frame of reference that you have been taught will serve you when in fact it doesn't, and tap instead into the infinite wisdom and intelligence of your heart.

This is not mushy stuff by any means – love can be fierce and wild, tempestuous and feisty. Love can move mountains and it is this very same energy, wisdom and power that we need to tap into in order to generate the life and the world we want to live in. It isn't fluffy and romantic, but comes, rather, with great clarity and directness and dignity. *Dance Your Way To The Top!* won't teach you how to 'do' leadership; rather, it will teach you how to flow into the fullness of who you are and be a leader in all your glory, whatever it is you spend your time doing, and transform from the *inside.*

True leadership is an inside job. If you're not at peace with yourself – and, like love, peace is neither weak nor mushy; it's strong and intensely powerful – if your relationships aren't authentic, if you're unable to tell your nearest and dearest from your heart exactly how you feel and what's going on for you, then you will be at war. You will continue to be at effect instead of at cause.

Leadership is about being at cause. How you lead always comes back to expanding your own personal capacity. Your ultimate business is as CEO of your own life – this is such an enormous privilege.

United as women leaders, we have more than just a possibility to make a difference. Women's circles are being created all over the globe as women are rediscovering and at last taking heed of those whispers from our ancestral energy and our DNA as they rise to the surface. Ancient wisdom from aeons past is calling us to now be who we really are, to be fully self-expressed. It's lack of self-expression and lack of authenticity that contributes to burnout as we try to tamp down and suppress our true nature.

We are being called, instead, to reawaken our true feminine energy. We are the mothers of men, and even if we're not biologically mothers ourselves, we need to teach the following generations – not by behaving like men but by honouring ourselves first and teaching them to honour us too. Because we teach other people how to treat us!

The only security we have in this uncertain world is if we create it ourselves in the knowledge that we are not powerless, but extraordinarily powerful as a group of women working together. I'm sorry to tell you but your fairy godmother isn't likely to turn up with her magic wand and make it all better, unless you become your *own* fairy godmother! Nor is that prince in shining armour going to come riding in on his white charger, no matter how often you dream that dream. We have to find the resources from within and become the mistresses of our own destinies – then and only then will the men come and support us.

Both the masculine and feminine together create our world. The energy that creates life comes from both sperm and egg. Just one on its own won't suffice, no matter how often some women may say that a world without men would be heavenly. Quite frankly, it would be hell.

> *"Synergy – the bonus that is achieved*
> *when things work together harmoniously."*

> Mark Twain

People often confuse feminine with being weak and submissive, but feminine energy is truly awesome and extraordinary. If you've ever given birth or seen a woman giving birth, you'll know that once she's committed, she has to see it through to the end! And there is nothing in nature as powerful as a mother bear!

> **What if it's time to stop being a 'nice' girl and revel in the**
> **magnificence of who you really are and celebrate that?**
> **What if this is the time to be a force of nature,**
> **to make the difference you so crave?**

The Feminine Leadership I am talking about is *inspired* leadership, conscious leadership for the greater good, that draws people in.

For years I've heard the term 'servant leadership' and seen both men and women collapse under the strain of eternal giving, constantly being '*in* service'. Leading from the front where you stand and dictate is no longer viable, while leading from behind induces fear. Being '*of* service' carries a totally different energy.

The New Paradigm is committed, conscious, aware, loving and softly powerful. It is inclusive, integrative, promotes a culture with more reverence for life, for the feminine aspect inside both genders. It embraces experiential learning, intuition, primordial wisdom and somatic intelligence. It is about being aligned with Life itself, a new perspective from which to live a meaningful and vibrant life, for everyone.

Chapter 5

What on Earth are You Doing?

One contributory factor of burnout is the stressful championing and pursuit of work that isn't what you know deep down inside you're here for. While I've heard many people saying that burnout is the most amazing event as it can lead to a new awakening, I've been there and done that, and if I can help you achieve that same awakening without the pain and devastation of burning out, then I'll sleep happily at night!

So what on this Earth *are* you doing?

The expression 'life-purpose' actually carries a very masculine energy, so now having grabbed your attention, I would like you to go more gently on yourself, and allow this to be in flow as you return to your authentic core essence.

Just to let you know, your life-purpose really is to be all you can be, to be your true self, allowing your unique gifts, your talents and your joy to rise to the surface, and to live from that perspective, as the best version of yourself, the real you. Imagine what a difference you'll make to the world when you live like that and how much you will influence others!

Many of us know that we are called to do something – we know we want to make a difference and do something meaningful with our life but can't quite work out what it is. This little exercise will help you to hone in on what is *really* important to you in this magical journey we call life, where your purpose is bigger than your own current circumstances. Let's call this your 'Inspiring Invincible Vision'.

Being an inspired visionary leader will take you to places you never even dreamed of, and is vital for both your personal and professional life. It will enable you to leave a legacy for your descendants and make what I refer to as a 'Dent in the Universe' for the good of man and womankind. What matters is that you have a dream.

Women in particular have an ability to look at things and see the difference they will make in seven generations, so if you create your 'Inspiring Invincible Vision' from this perspective, it will outlive you by possibly hundreds of years. Now wouldn't that make a difference as to how you view your everyday life?

If you can't complete the lists immediately, just relax and allow the answers to rise gently to the surface. This doesn't mean that you have to take the world by storm by being the new Prime Minister or President or the new Nobel Prize winner; for you it might be about being the best you can be as mother, as a chocolate maker, as a cleaner, or as the manager of a team. Notice what excites you – stay open to possibilities. If you set your vision too low, you will end up living a life of quiet desperation.

This is about awakening the genius self that lies dormant within. Later you'll learn how to bring your vision into being, but in a different way from how you may have been taught to date.

List 1

What do you *really* most want out of life?

Make a list of at least 10 things:

1._____

2._____

3._____

4._____

5._____

6._____

7._____

8._____

9._____

10._____

List 2

What do you most want to see happen in the world/on the planet? What is most important to you here? Including others in your vision gives it far more possibility of coming to fruition because it is as if Life gets on side with you to support you.

Make a list of at least 10 things:

1._____

2._____

3._____

4._____

5._____

6._____

7._____

8._____

9._____

10._____

List 3

What is different about you – those things that you believe make you unique and special, or which other people comment on and acknowledge you for?

Make a list of at least 10 things:

1._____

2._____

3._____

4._____

5._____

6._____

7._____

8._____

9._____

10._____

List 4

What are you good at that you also really enjoy doing? What makes your heart sing? Whatever this is, it needs to be intensely meaningful and core to your identity, where you are happy and passionate about what you do.

Make a list of at least 10 things:

1._____

2._____

3._____

4._____

5._____

6._____

7._____

8._____

9._____

10._____

Now go through each of your lists carefully and select from each list your number one priority. If you could only pick one from each list, which would it be? Take time over your selection, as this is important.

List 1._____

List 2._____

List 3._____

List 4._____

Now this is where the magic begins: complete the following sentence, using your number one priority from each list. It may not make perfect sense grammatically, but you should get a strong sense of the meaning and how it resonates with you.

I will (List 4) _____

_____using my (List 3)_____

_____ to accomplish (List 2)_____

_____and in doing so, achieve (List 1)_____

_____

And now, when you focus on what really inspires you, when you have a big enough 'why', and take action by taking just the first steps towards achieving it, the path will reveal itself to you more and more.

"When you are inspired by some great purpose, some extraordinary project, all your thoughts break their bonds. Your mind transcends limitations, your consciousness expands in every direction, and you find yourself in a new, great, and wonderful world. Dormant forces,

faculties, and talents become alive, and you discover yourself to be a greater person by far than you ever dreamed yourself to be."

Patanjali – Indian teacher from around 400 BCE
often referred to as the Father of Yoga

I want you to now bring up that vision so you can picture it perfectly (as if it is already accomplished) in glorious technicolor and in the finest detail possible, as if you could almost reach out and touch it. Research suggests that people who can think in pictures and hold on to those pictures in their mind, together with an intensity of positive emotion, have far greater possibilities of success than those who are only able to come from their feeling centre.

Now bring in any sounds associated with that vision. Now whatever you are feeling physically as you look at it, and ramp up how you are feeling emotionally. Maybe there are tastes and smells associated with your Invincible Vision too.

Keep going through your Invincible Vision on a daily basis so it comes to the forefront of your mind, keeping you on track, excited, enthusiastic and so you bounce out of bed in the morning *knowing it is already accomplished at some place in time and space* – even if you can't see it yet.

A word of caution: some of the brightest flames who know what their life-purpose is and pursue it passionately and relentlessly, letting nothing else get in their way, are often the first to burn out, as they lose connection with their body's wisdom and so push through, regardless of the consequences. I'll show you how to avoid this, by tapping into your inner resources and dancing your way through, because this is about getting your Invincible Vision imprinted on to the deeper part of your mind so that your unconscious mind leads the way inexorably towards it. So rather than you pushing towards it, it almost becomes effortless.

My intention in the next few chapters is to ensure that you approach your Inspiring Invincible Vision in a way that is more in keeping with your feminine energy, both honouring your deep desires and making your difference in the world. But before we do, we need to look at what's stopping you.

Chapter 6

The Feminine Addiction Trap That is Killing Your Career

So what's holding you back from stepping into your magnificence as a leader in your own right? Is it fear? Is it that feeling of just not quite being good enough, ready enough or qualified enough? Do you say to yourself: "I'm just waiting until I...?"

This is such a typical response for women. While men just grab opportunities by the horns whether they fit the criteria or not, women hold back for all sorts of reasons. I used to call them excuses, but having worked with thousands of women over the years, I'm now boldly, and with great love, calling them: 'Feminine Addictions'.

Many women are completely unaware that they're sabotaging their health, wealth and happiness through these dangerous addictions. And, while some may not be strictly classified as such in medical terms, the behaviours are so strong and frequently employed that they soon begin to form their own well-worn neural-pathways in the brain, becoming a learned behaviour pattern. And they will not go away until they are addressed.

"Feminine Addictions? Who, me? Oh you mean like handbags and chocolate," is a typical response. Yes, that'll do for starters, but what else? Then, as I dig deeper, out come the confessions: snuffling your way through the contents of sugar tubes in coffee shops; buying more and more 'stuff' off the internet that just caught your eye; racking up credit card debt; taking just one more course that gives you another qualification; 'just one more' glass of red wine after work; hour after hour spent on social media catching up with people you probably don't even know; unfulfilling sex with the wrong people; the warmth, wellbeing and relief induced by over-the-counter painkillers; yet another diet as the last one didn't work; the latest anti-aging cream used by all the film stars, and so on and so forth.

When we go deeper still, what emerges are the life-sapping *emotional behaviours* which are repeated over and over again until they become wired in the neural pathways of the brain like the Tube lines beneath the streets of London.

More often than not, you know you're doing it, but because everyone else around you is doing it too, it somehow becomes acceptable. Other times, you're unaware how much a behaviour has seeped into your unconscious and that you've been surreptitiously hijacked by it, so that it inadvertently affects everything you do and every interaction with other people, stealing your life into the bargain.

More importantly who would you be without these behaviours, and how would you be able to live in this hectic, modern world?

More and more millennial women are falling into the 'Feminine Addiction Trap' in a desperate attempt to keep up with the ever-increasing whirlwind that society dictates. However, it's not just that generation who have been brought up to expect more, demand more and think they're invincible. You've been taught that you can have it all: "Because you're worth it!"

So as a result, you go out there with all guns firing, only to discover at some stage that you've run out of silver bullets – you're exhausted, unwell and wondering why you can't make the grade. But let me break the bubble of illusion – it has nothing to do with being worthy!

What start as habits often end up as addictive behaviours that keep you stuck on a relentless treadmill, where you feel your life will fall apart if you stop what you're doing. So if coffee to wake you up and pills to help you sleep, alcohol to relax you, and beating yourself up when you fail to reach the increasingly high standards you've set yourself, if a relationship falls apart and you're in despair, or you fail to get a promotion despite staying late in the office, and you have enough unanswered emails to create an encyclopedia, all sound familiar, read on – this concerns you!

In my work with hundreds of men and women, I've discovered that women win hands down in the non-resourceful behaviour stakes, while men often look on in bemusement saying: "Why on earth would you do that to yourself?" What started out as copying men's behaviour in many instances has turned against us because of our biology.

Let's be very frank here – women do not have the same biological make-up as men and therefore we can't treat our bodies in the same way. If you've been drinking to keep up with the boys, or exercising manically to get a six-pack or competing in an Iron-Man triathlon, or working harder to justify your existence, chances are that at some stage your body will rebel.

56

While at many levels men and women can seem astoundingly similar (and we've spent the last few decades trying to prove this very point!), women have less adrenaline than men and, what's more, we run out of it sooner. Our bodies are designed differently and for very good reasons – we're the birth-givers, for goodness sake! Generally, we have less long-term endurance and stamina unless it's a matter of life or death, although in the pain stakes we win hands down – just look at a woman in labour! Our brains are wired differently and our hormones respond in a different way. And we need more sleep. Is it little wonder that we burn out so easily? Your female body was made to run on 200,000 year-old software, and no matter how much you try to beat men at their own game, this particular software hasn't had an upgrade yet.

As an Executive and also Relationship and Intimacy Coach and Hypnotherapist, I've had clients present with all manner of issues from wanting to quit smoking, to problems with alcohol, anorexia and bulimia, body dysmorphic disorder and obesity, lack of self-esteem, lack of confidence, sleep problems, Obsessive Compulsive Disorder, stress, panic attacks, fears and phobias, sexual disorders, relationship issues, infertility, financial problems – the list is endless. But what is going on deep down?

Feminine Addictions happen when you lose touch with your instincts and your authenticity, and when you stop living from your highest values (more of this later). You're born with instincts – innate hereditary reactions that have a powerful influence on behaviour, such as responding to natural hunger, sexual needs, privacy, identity, and so much more. You have an instinct for life, for survival: your eyes and what you see, your ears and what you hear, your nose and what you smell, your mouth and what you taste, your sense of touch and your 'second brain' – your gut – instinctively keep you on track. But our so-called 'civilised' society has bashed the instinct out of us so that we no longer heed its messages. Society blocks, disorganises and perverts our natural instincts and as we follow its dictates, so we also override them.

We've raped the planet: taken its oils, minerals and gems, poured concrete all over the earth, chopped down its lungs (the trees and the rainforest,) polluted its life blood (its lakes, seas and rivers) and corrupted her fertility (the soil in which our plants grow, as well as the genetic modification of crops.)

We've been taught to look down on what used to be called 'heathen' people and 'uncivilised' tribal developing world peoples, regarding them as primitive and uneducated because they live much more by their instincts, but the human race would have died out if your ancestors hadn't listened to theirs!

In fact, the human race is in desperate danger of dying out very rapidly with its 21st century dis-eases, lack of true connection with our human bodies and the abuse of our beloved planet, unless we re-connect with our instincts as the foundation for life.

As a woman, you're even more likely to be sensitively attuned to your body because of your menstrual cycle. However, even that has often been hijacked by pills and potions, as society has done everything it can to dishonour and disown those parts of us that make us intrinsically female.

Recently it was announced that the number of women over 50 giving birth has just doubled! So when their son or daughter wants picking up from a party at midnight at the age of 20, the mother will be 70!! And it's unlikely they'll be around to enjoy the wonder and playfulness of being a grandmother. While I totally empathise with the instinct for motherhood, where has rationale and common sense gone? Just because we *can* doesn't mean we *should*!

As a result of my research and experience with clients, I've come up with seven different categories for my Feminine Addictions list:

1. The Overs

2. The Unders

3. Body Hatred

4. Addicted to the Impossible

5. The Love Bug

6. Virtual Addiction

7. Minding the Gap

I have a whole methodology for breaking through the Feminine Addiction Trap, but for now, as you read through the following lists, please do yourself and your body the favour of acknowledging all the places where you could put a check mark and go: "Yes, this is me!"

Get clarity on what you need support and help for, so you are no longer dictated to by these life-sapping thoughts and behaviours. Feminine Addictions are the way the body and mind wave a red flag at you to attract your attention, to remind you that you are not living by your highest values, not living authentically, not living a life of meaning!

Feminine Addiction No. 1: 'The Overs'

Over-work; Overwhelm; Over-spending; Over-exercise; Over-indulgence;
Over-masculine; Over-analytical; Over-eating; Over-doing; Over-busy;
Over-dramatic; Over-powering; Over-conscientious; Over-controlling;
Over-organised; Over-obsessive (OCD); Over-stretched; Over-thinking;
Over-worrying; Over-giving; Over-spending; Over-anxious; Over-cautious

Many of the women I've coached over the years, either individually or in workshops, present with these problems, turning up in their immaculate business suits, beautifully painted acrylic nails and killer heels, wondering why they can't have an orgasm or why they can't get pregnant, or indeed, get to the top.

Most of this exhausting list compels you to push your energy outwards, to strive, to struggle, to try harder, to gird your loins in order to get out there in the world, to fight and defend. It's very masculine energy and one which in time will take its toll on your precious female body-chemistry and psyche, your vitality, your relationships (particularly intimacy) and also the way in which you show up in the world.

If you're an 'Over', then you need to be aware that this is *learned* behaviour, employing our 'emergency' male energy from our special reserves, as we've seen other seemingly successful women live their lives this way and feel we have to do the same in order to get to the top, much against the wisdom of our bodies.

I have enough experience in this area to award myself a Ph.D. in overwhelm, overwork, over-busyness, overdoing and overmasculinization. So much so that I've written a whole book on this subject – *The Essence of Womanhood – Re-awakening the Authentic Feminine.*

When I look through my photo album, most photos are of me up a ladder in paint-splattered jeans, on the roof with the builders, wielding a chainsaw as I chopped down trees, or in a business suit with power-shoulders, killer heels and war paint, ready for battle. The only other photos are of me looking totally unkempt in a dressing gown, feeding my babies. I acted out this particular addiction very well, and have not only studied the reasons behind my behaviour, but have found solutions too, some of which I'll be sharing with you later.

If you're an 'Over', I can pretty much guarantee that you'll burn out at some stage – and it will be messy, painful, bad timing, inconvenient and devastating on many levels and will also take more than just a few months to heal.

I know, because I've been there, and teetered on the edge again more than once. My 'Overs' left me with a weakened immune system, where I had to give up the fight and completely surrender to what was going on.

I trust that as you continue to read through this book and take notice of what I'm sharing with you, commit to doing the exercises (rather than thinking that just reading about them will solve the issues) and incorporate them into everyday life, that I can spare you experiencing what I went through.

- Burnout is a breakdown of the energy system of the body where vital minerals are depleted or burned out and replaced by toxic metals. Healing involves rebuilding body chemistry because it is a physical condition. However, psychological stress may be a cause too, and burnout can affect your emotions and behaviour. Recovery may involve improving emotions and dealing with psychological issues.

- Many in burnout hold full-time jobs. They may appear in good health. However, they're often desperately tired or stressed. They may require stimulants in order to keep going. Some bury themselves in their work to forget how tired they feel.

- Simply put, your body/mind system is completely interrelated. So every emotion that you experience is accompanied by a corresponding secretion from the endocrine system. 'The Overs' produce massive amounts of rapid-acting adrenaline and slower-acting cortisol from the adrenal glands. These enter your system and if not used up by your body in a physical 'fight, flight or freeze' response, continue to circulate in your system, eventually degenerating your organs, particularly your liver and kidneys, and lead to adrenal fatigue.

The stress hormone, cortisol, is Public Health Enemy Number One. Scientists have known for years that elevated cortisol levels interfere with learning and memory, lower immune function and bone density, increase weight gain, blood pressure, cholesterol, heart disease... and much, much more.

Chronic stress and elevated cortisol levels also increase the risk of decreased resilience, mental illness and lower life expectancy, together with Feminine Addiction No. 2, 'The Unders', which includes depression.

To compensate, the body produces the antidote, noradrenalin. This induces a feeling of euphoria, wellbeing and analgesia which makes you feel good initially. In extreme cases, people become 'adrenaline junkies' – hooked on the buzz of extreme stress and its relief. Clear-cut examples of these are often journalists and people working in the media, city brokers, and others working in the financial industry. This in turn can lead to a lifestyle of extremes often leading to Feminine Addiction No. 7, 'Minding the Gap'.

'The Overs' are more inclined to take 'uppers' such as amphetamines or cocaine to keep going, and 'downers' (tranquillisers, sleeping pills or opiates) to get sleep or rest. These all degenerate the nervous system, lowering the body's immunity and harming vital organs.

My invitation here is to let go of what is not working and surrender to the wisdom of your feminine energy, learn how to truly relax, not just your body but your mind as well, and get help to reprogramme your unconscious mind so that it works *for* you and not *against* you. I can assure you that is not weak and feeble, but feisty, juicy and potent.

Feminine Addiction No. 2: 'The Unders'

Under-achieving; Under-valued; Under-paid; Low self-esteem; Why me?
Emotional addictions; Victimhood; 'Poor Me' Syndrome; Addicted to pain
and suffering; Comparing Yourself to Others; Self-sabotage; Self-judgement;
Conformity; Fear of being found out; The Imposter Syndrome; Depression;
People-pleasing; Self-Sacrifice; Good Girl/Nice Girl/Doing-My-Duty
Syndrome; Feeling under-qualified; Never-enough Syndrome;
Next Bright-Shiny Object Syndrome

Hormones from the endocrine system are implicated here too, such as those produced by the thyroid gland that can affect mood, food metabolism and sexual function. Also involved are higher levels of cortisol and low levels of testosterone.

The origins of these behaviours tend to stem from childhood programming about how little girls should behave, (sugar and spice and all things nice!) but may also have come just from overhearing an unfortunate remark by chance, spoken by a parent or teacher when your unconscious mind was open, such as when you were happy, upset or engrossed in watching a film.

It's all about not feeling good enough – a general lack of self-worth, a lack of faith in who you are and how much difference you really do make. My belief is that depression is a squashing of the spirit, from not being fully self-expressed or allowing yourself to be authentic, so that you hide behind masks and false personas. You will find out about these in a later chapter.

As women, we carry much of this in our genetic make-up, due to a generalised but insidious lack of self-worth having been thrust down our throats for generation after generation, particularly from organised religion. It has become embedded in our ancestral heritage, literally in our DNA, but this doesn't mean that we have to react to it.

My dance with 'The Unders' was very much linked to my perception as to what it meant to be a female, through watching my mother who squashed her own personal desires by obeying my loving but often domineering father's wishes. In fact, I remember at one stage thinking of my mother as a second-class citizen and deciding that that was what it was like to be a woman – after all she was beautiful and elegant and she was my role model. I didn't know any different. I knew I was expected to get a job until I married and had children.

My brother, on the other hand, was treated differently, and I always felt he was superior to me as, indeed, were all members of the male species. So, I did 'people-pleasing' very well (which actually doesn't work, no matter how hard you try!) along with 'Next-Bright-Shiny-Object Syndrome' (feeling that the next course I took or product I bought would make me feel better about myself).

On the one hand we're taught that we're mere specks of insignificant dust on a little rock in the vastness of space, and on the other hand, you only have to look around the world to find magnificent examples of both men and women who have had such an Invincible Vision that they've changed the world.

When you respond in a different way and learn to dance in the moment, with awe, wonder and appreciation, and dare to live full out, life will start to give you very different feedback.

My invitation here is to step into the fullness of who you really are, put aside all these disempowering behaviours, get out of your own way and rediscover who you truly are at your core, in your essence. You will be amazed and enthralled by who shows up!

The world is only changed by people who don't conform...

Feminine Addiction No.3: Body Hatred

Obsessive dieting; Fashion victim; Self-judgement; Fear of getting older;
Eating disorders; Anorexia nervosa; Bulimia; Lack of self-care; Sleep
disorders; Body-armour – physical and emotional; Plastic surgery; Botox; etc.

Have you ever stood in front of a mirror and criticised what you saw? Very few women have never done so, as we're continually being compared to beautiful models, airbrushed to within an inch of their existence by a whole team of make-up artists, a tribe of clothes designers and a truckload of photographic visual-effects specialists.

How can we possibly compare ourselves to them? I recently discovered that the main model in my favourite mail-order catalogue is 6'2" tall and a size 8! I felt relieved, vindicated, and at the same time deeply frustrated. And this is what we are being sold every single day, along with the next DIE-T (notice the first three letters here!) face-cream to remove our 'unsightly' wrinkles, and pills to stop us aging.

The number of celebrities who've undergone the knife, and not only are unrecognisable, but have lost the features and expressions that made them so intrinsically human in the first place, horrifies me. I've met so many women whose smile doesn't reach their eyes, and they do this in the name of beauty! There are certain states in the US where body sculpting is so much part of the culture that most of the women look the same. That doesn't bode well for finding a true intimate relationship based on love and respect.

It saddens me that we can't enjoy the process of aging gracefully (or disgracefully!) because I hate to tell you, you are going to grow old and you are going to die. Don't regret growing older – it's a privilege denied to many!

Sleep disorders became my addiction – I decided that if Prime Minister Maggie Thatcher could run a country on five hours sleep a day, then I could run my life on that too. After all, sleep seemed such a waste of time when life was so short and there were so many things to be done. So I fell into the pattern of burning the candle at both ends, ignoring the protests my body and mind made when I was tired, as I valiantly pushed on through.

Sleep is now being hailed as the most important thing we can do to regenerate our looks, our hormones, our health and our vitality. My invitation here is to fall in love with your body so your body has the opportunity to fall in love with you. Loving your body is not restricted to an emotion. It is an ongoing daily activity, not a passive event. After all, you wouldn't treat your best friend the way you treat yourself, would you?

Allowing your true essence and beauty to shine through is the key, as these are what are most appealing to everyone whose path you cross. And smile!

Feminine Addiction No 4: Addicted to the Impossible

*Perfectionism (body, plastic surgery, fashion); Conformity; Status;
Getting to the Top of the Ladder at Work; Money and Lifestyle;
Fear of Failure/Fear of Success; Control; OCD (Obsessive Compulsive Disorder);
Perfect Business; Perfect Wife; Perfect Mother; Perfect Hostess; Perfect Lover;
Perfect House; Perfect Children; Perfect Holidays; Perfect Partner;
Perfect Sex-Life; Perfect Everything*

Perfectionism, judgement, discrimination and control are all masculine energies that have been handed down mainly via religious sects over the centuries, and more recently within business. As a result, women were deemed to be flawed creatures, and we have continued to buy into it at an unconscious level, hook, line and sinker.

Can you keep a secret? You're already perfect enough!

Perfectionism is synonymous with being an over-achiever. Like some of the other Feminine Addictions, being 'Addicted to the Impossible' induces cortisol, adrenaline and noradrenalin to flood through your body with their disastrous consequences. Unreal self-expectations lead to self-blame from inevitable poor results, leading to a reduction in productivity, forcing you to repeat the cycle, only this time demanding even higher standards.

I did this well too, certainly in the stakes of having a perfect house (we had 24 rooms including out-houses and glasshouses, all in a state of Edwardian dishevelment) and I was continually up ladders decorating, saying to myself: "It will all be so much better when this room is finished … and this one … and this one." By the time I was halfway through, the first one needed redoing. I was intent on being the perfect hostess, from time to time cooking five-course meals from scratch for 20 people; trying to be the Perfect Lover(!), the Perfect Mother, giving my three children quality time, having a perfect organic garden and running my own horticulture business on top as well!

Fear of failure/fear of success loomed large. What if I failed? What if I were successful? Would I lose my friends/my husband? Too many stories to tell you here, but in short, it didn't go well!

> ***"Dear Human.
> You've got it all wrong.
> You didn't come here to master unconditional love.***

That is where you came from and where you'll return.
You came here to learn personal love.
Universal love. Messy love. Sweaty love. Crazy love. Broken love.
Whole love. Infused with divinity. Lived through the grace of stumbling.
Demonstrated through the beauty of ... messing up. Often.
You didn't come here to be perfect. You already are.
You came here to be gorgeously human.
Flawed and fabulous.
And then to rise again into remembering.
But unconditional love? Stop telling that story.
Love, in truth, doesn't need ANY other adjectives.
It doesn't require modifiers. It doesn't require the condition of perfection.
It only asks that you show up. And do your best. That you stay present
and feel fully. That you shine and fly and laugh and cry and hurt and
heal and fall
and get back up and play and work and live and die as YOU.
It's enough.
It's plenty."

Included here by kind permission of Courtney A. Walsh

Here I invite you to dance with what is, to celebrate the successes and release the failures; to enjoy the dreams and release those which for some reason may not be possible in this lifetime; to express all those emotions which keep you stuck; to play full-out without self-criticism; to appreciate the splendour, magic and awesomeness of creation, and to let go of all that is not you, in order to reveal the best version of you that you can be.

This is about giving birth to your Self so that *all* thoughts are finally allowed expression. All those feelings we used to label as 'negative' or 'dark' or 'dangerous' are finally given voice and expression, allowed to breathe and rest and be fully themselves.

We sometimes forget that these are also part of the rich tapestry of who we are as our authentic selves, as we rush around trying in vain to fix them.

Feminine Addiction No.5: The Love Bug

*Flying Solo - I can do it all myself! The Disney Effect - Addicted to Romance;
Sex in the City - any man will do! Desperately Seeking ... sperm!
The Lone Ranger; The Merry Widow/Embittered Divorcee*

Many women under the age of 40 have been taught to never trust a man. So they go it alone, building armour of self-protection and self-defence around themselves, and then wonder why they're unhappy. Those of us who have trodden the earth a little longer know that life is impossible on your own – you need a tribe of loving supportive friends and people you care about around you, to ask for others' advice, to give and receive in turn.

As a Relationship and Intimacy Coach, I also feel it's time we learned to reclaim our own creative sexual energy that we've denied ourselves so often in this throw-away shallow society, and to reconnect with, and rediscover, our love for that sacred, divine part of ourselves that we've cheapened. When we take on the same energy as a man, we lose that intimacy, passion, desire, tenderness and creativity in our personal relationships. Many women's illnesses are caused through a lack of deep sexual fulfilment and a dumbing-down of their effervescence, radiance and natural beauty.

And how would it be if we learned to love our men more deeply, to engage with them at all levels, to show them the beauty of the world and of life so they spent more time making love rather than war?

I'm pleased to say that this is one addiction I didn't get too hooked on, although what I call 'The Disney Effect', waiting for my knight – not only in shining armour and on a white charger, an eco-warrior but also with lots of money, delightful, a good sense of humour, sexy, adoring and passionate – took up rather a lot of time, thought and wishful thinking!

I became a Relationship and Intimacy Coach and Sex Therapist as a result of my Executive coaching. Almost every time a client came to me with business challenges, whether men or women, within ten minutes what emerged more often than not was a problem in their intimacy and home life. Once this was addressed, the knock-on effect was astounding, affecting their health, happiness and ability to earn money, and particularly the way they showed up at work.

Here I invite you to dive deep into the heart of love, sex and intimacy and to dance with your gorgeous, juicy sexuality, that yin/yang energy of creation, for *this* is where your origins lie. Being the leader of your own life here awakens your instincts fully and keeps you safe, healthy and full of joy and vitality.

Feminine Addiction No.6: Virtual Living

Internet Obsession; Phone Addiction; Email Overwhelm; Social Media Addiction - FB/Twitter/ Pinterest/LinkedIn and so on; Technology; On-Line Games/Video Games; On-line Gambling

Virtual living means you are not actually living in this world at all, but living under the influence and programming of other people who have a vested interest in keeping you addicted, and indeed employ very underhand methods to ensure that you are kept hooked. Social media addiction and addiction to the virtual world where you have 4,900 friends, most of whom you've never met nor have a real relationship with, is not only a major distraction, but also leaves you feeling empty, dissociated and devoid of true human contact, combined with a fear of missing out.

While being part of a group on-line can be incredibly supportive if you're suffering in some areas of your life (and I know that but for my Facebook friends, I would have gone under when I was nursing my mother in her final months), to hold someone in your arms physically, where you soothe and are soothed by their presence and the love that surges from their heart through their hands and into your body so you can relax, melt and just be, is wonderfully healing and regenerating.

My ex-husband was involved in advertising, and so I became aware first-hand of just how manipulative the media can be, both in what they show you and what they leave out. At that time too, I was also a production assistant in a film production company, where the 'missed takes' were edited out and dropped on to the studio floor in order to create a more perfect product.

Later, when I had my own horticulture business and was being interviewed by major newspapers and magazines, I had to fight my corner when photographs were being taken, as the 'poetic licence' employed just didn't make sense: plants were grouped together for photographic purposes which in their normal environment wouldn't have had a hope of survival. So what you see in the media isn't necessarily what is there!

Babies without human touch die. Adults without loving human touch suffer, mentally, emotionally and physically. Thinking that connection on-line equals true connection brings something alien into our lives as living, breathing human beings.

Here I invite you to connect again with the deepest part of you with all its dreams and hopes, your love and desires, your imaginary world, so you can manifest these imaginary aspects into reality – your creative self into being. And then to connect with real people, dancing together to create something that is life transforming. I can't begin to describe the relief and the surge of excitement you'll feel, as you discover a part of you that's been hidden for so long.

Feminine Addiction No. 7: Mind the Gap

Alcohol/ Binge-drinking;
Nicotine/Illegal Drugs; Caffeine/Chocolate/Sodas; Comfort Eating;
Addiction to Fat/Sugar/Salt/Carbohydrates;
Prescribed Drugs/Over-The-Counter Medicines;
Thrill-seeking/Endorphin Highs

In London, when the underground trains pull into the station, a voice comes over the loudspeakers, saying, "Mind The Gap." This is the gap between the step and the platform edge, and is such an appropriate analogy for that hole, that gap, that void, that emptiness that we feel we need to fill when something vital is missing from our lives.

I used to smoke like a chimney when I was younger. Lots of us did – it was a rite of passage. Then I had a problem with Valium, which was prescribed when I was severely ill, so I got by on a haze of disconnection, feeling as if my life was a blurred cinema-screen playing out in front of me. From there, in my early twenties, I drifted into fine wines and boozy business lunches so that alcohol became part of my daily existence – not in an excessive way – but certainly seldom a day went by without at least one large glass of something to take the edge off the stress before the sun went down. Many years later during another severe illness, I was prescribed painkillers in order to sleep and to get through the day, together with bottles of liquid morphine.

My personal 'drugs' of choice since childhood were unusually milk and Marmite (a yeast-based product which people either love or hate but which many British babies are brought up on). I was effectively a 'milk-aholic'. I couldn't get by without a pint of the cold stuff from the fridge that made me high and kept me satisfied, and once the effects wore off, nothing else would quench my thirst. Without it, severe depression and withdrawal symptoms set in.

What possibly started out as an emotional comfort turned in on itself and became a major allergen for me – I was actually highly allergic to milk and it made me very ill, but trying to come off it was at least as bad as stopping an addictive drug. I also couldn't travel without my pot of Marmite and constantly had my finger in the jar to lick off its dark, salty deliciousness. As a result, I suffered very badly from Candida.

So food may not be as obvious as other addictions, but any food that you can't live without can have an adverse effect, not only chemically and physiologically, but psychologically too. You will have noticed too that we are learning more and more about the physical and mental problems associated with sugar.

Here I invite you to fill the gap instead with pleasure, with abundance of life, with adventure, with grace, with peace, with ease, with excitement, with joy, with truth, with tenderness, with friendship, with a nurturing touch, and with a deep connection with Life where you become the vessel through which Life expresses itself.

On a lighter note, go to YouTube and look up *'Bob Newhart – Stop It!'* He has a simple remedy for much repetitive behaviour, which you'll laugh at because his cure is totally plausible. Essentially, just stop doing it – get out of your own way!

It's not necessary to delve into the deep, darkest depths to discover the cause; you just need to name and shame what's going on without beating yourself up about it! And take remedial action from there.

Now, why do we do these awful things to ourselves?

People develop addictions in order to shield themselves from intolerably painful feelings. However, any addiction always creates harmful, often ignored consequences, so the sooner you deal with these, the sooner you'll be able to return to living your life fully. You may find it enlightening to discover who or what 'did' it to you, but it's not essential. At some level it may not even belong to you. It may be part of your genetic make-up to have a propensity for some of these behaviours.

Other times it's learned behaviour from people around you, not just your caregivers, but the people you hang out with. In the same way we can pick up a virus and it morphs inside us, so too, we pick up behaviours, thinking patterns and disturbances in our energy that didn't originate with us. As women we're very sensitive to our surroundings, often picking up the emotions and feelings of others. This is a natural part of who we are, built into the qualities of being a mother, a nurturer, a caretaker, a lover.

If you think that's a bit far-fetched, think how often you get on the train or tube feeling good, and come off it feeling miserable or exhausted: it's not just the lack of oxygen, but the energy fields you're sharing with other people who, for whatever reason, may be feeling down, and their misery or ailment sticks to you like Velcro. This is not fanciful, head-in-the-clouds stuff – it's a scientific fact. Misery is contagious! But so too is happiness.

In order to heal unconscious wounding you need to allow the expression of the emotion of the experience that originally caused the wound in the first place. Because we learn, very early on, *not* to express our anger, hurt, upset, displeasure, annoyance, irritation, sadness, grief, fear, hopelessness or desperation, we are literally a sea of unexpressed emotion. We *have* to obey our parents; we have no choice, as we are dependent on them for our survival. We cannot live out our emotions, as they are designed for fight, flight or freeze. We have to be civilised, to be polite, to be well behaved and always, always in control. And so we become nice, good girls and boys, seething with anger and resentment underneath, bulging with grief and sadness and replete with fears, both real and imaginary.

If you think that sounds scary, please go back to my Letter to the Men, where I gave myself permission to feel and express fully how I felt, from the depths of my guts. You will realise the power of this in the later chapter *Dancing With the Dark Side*. Releasing that justified anger in a safe environment was the most thrilling, energising, enlightening and sexy thing I'd done in a long while, deeply pleasurable at a primordial level, and left me feeling empowered and released, energised and ready to move on and create.

I don't promise you a pain-free existence because it seems that pain, challenges and the overcoming of major obstacles are also necessary along the journey through life in order for us to emerge stronger and wiser. Leaders in fact seek out challenges that inspire them. If you don't, life will fill you up with challenges that don't inspire you!

I do, however, promise you a feeling of self-reliance and confidence when you do the exercises in this book; an experience of wholeness; a deeper connection with that 'higher' part of yourself which remains unseen that you may call your soul or your spirit; an expansion into the 'more' that you are seeking, and fulfilment at a profound level which you can share with others. If you are truly a leader, I know you will relate to this.

These symptoms are nothing more than guides to lead us back to meaning.

So when you say, "There must be more to life than this," or "I want more," let this be the pathway that guides you to opening up as yet unexpressed elements of your life.

Chapter 7

Your Female Brain

As women we've been taught that we have to think in similar ways to men (with logic, reasoning, decisions, computations, judgements and criticism) in order to keep up with them, but this is at the expense of our knowingness, our instincts and our intuition, which as a result have been grossly devalued. Actually, they've been judged, criticised and seen as limitations!

But these masculine behaviours that we've adopted have kept us stuck – we still live in a world that isn't in tune with the earth and how she evolves, creates and grows.

In the human foetus, the default sex is female. So much for Adam's rib and all that malarkey, as genetically, males are modified females! All foetuses are female until around the sixth week of gestation when a surge in testosterone, which starts small and then increases rapidly together with other pre-determined chromosome factors (please forgive the simplification here) cause a change in the sexual organs if the baby is to be a boy. This huge testosterone surge hits the brain, killing cells in the communication centre and growing them in the sex and aggression centre. So testosterone is vital for healthy development in males, but as females we don't need so much of it. However, living and behaving like men causes more testosterone to stream through our bodies – yet another contributing factor to burnout.

Some women have more testosterone in their system, dependent on their mother's lifestyle and habits when pregnant, and in their first two years of life. This epigenetic imprinting affects our whole lives unless we actively change our brain circuitry, delving into the unconscious mind and assisting it in rewiring, as this book is intended to do, for your own happiness, fulfilment and life-enhancement.

In the first decade of the 21st century, we women have often looked upon men as just hairy versions of ourselves, trying to coerce them into behaving more like us, resulting in many men having a hard time with their own identity. They're both afraid of the power of their intrinsic maleness and also afraid of losing their status. Many men are living with lowered testosterone levels which is vital for maleness, not only by behaving more like women themselves(!) but also because of hormones in medicines, livestock foods, chemical waste and plastics which seep into the food chain. On the other hand, we women have also adopted more testosterone through our behaviour and become more like men, ending up in a homogenous mess! There isn't room in this book to discuss this further, but just talk to a group of men and you'll discover their problems are almost as big as ours!

As a result of this dichotomy, we have more vicious wars, more religious fundamentalism, more violence and degradation towards women, more pornography and more paedophilia. Unfortunately, the list goes on…

Nature in her brilliance has designed us to procreate successfully – evolution only cares about reproduction and the care of the young. This is why male and female need to work together to create a whole, and why we need an integration of the masculine and feminine principles to create harmony. Just operating from one perspective will not work. And this applies to every aspect of life.

If we look at a list of inventions and creations that men have brought to this world, it looks as though women haven't had much of an input. But women's input has actually been remarkable, with queens and warrior women, inventors, athletes, pioneers, spies, soldiers, courtesans, scientists, poets, painters, writers and priests and much more. Some of the stories I've read about in our her-story as women have made me weep… with horror, and yet with joy and pride, too. No one in those far-flung times had told women that they were physically weak, emotionally unstable, illogical and inferior to men!

Historically, women mainly provided supplies of food, and we as gatherers developed agriculture, which in turn led to animal domestication. We invented cooking – we invented pots. So we were the hearth around which the early stages of civilisation developed. As a result, language was probably invented by women, too – the language of communication. It used to be said that women use around 20,000 words a day as opposed to men's use of 7,000. The truth seems to be that men use more words at work and women use more words at home. Whatever the facts, women are relational beings – this is how we've survived.

We relax by doing 'girly stuff' with other women, by talking intimately together, whether one-to-one or in groups. This use of relational behaviour activates the pleasure centres in our brain – it gives us a major dopamine and oxytocin rush – all those bonding hormones that are produced by the sharing of secrets and being together. This is the biggest, fattest, juiciest neurological reward we can experience other than an orgasm!

The emotional memory centre is bigger in women, so communication, connection, emotional sensitivity and responsiveness become our driving force and also determine our hierarchy of values.

Conflict on the other hand, sets into motion a cascade of negative chemical reactions, which create fear, upset and loss. The stress hormone cortisol takes over as we lose serotonin, oxytocin and dopamine. Psychological stress of conflict registers more deeply in certain areas of the female brain. The fight or flight mechanism isn't as heightened in women as historically we wouldn't have won because our frames are smaller than men's, which is why our tendency is to tend and befriend. It's also why we rely more on social networks for support and friendship.

So too, while being single-minded worked well for our menfolk as they went off on hunting forays to kill meat for the tribe, we had to have greater diffuse awareness, keeping an eye out for the snake in the grass, the poisoned berries or the sneaky woman who might have stolen not only our food, but also our protector, our man! Rejection and being left alone could have meant death for our cave woman ancestors.

The very fact that you're reading this book means that your forebears learned to play the game, to be fluid, to be aggressive when necessary and to fit in. And this is how we still are today – we've scarcely changed one iota in the last few thousand years. Lack of vital support is still terrifying to a woman, while self-esteem is partly sustained by the ability to maintain relationships with others.

To put it very simply, the *corpus collosum* – the bridge of nerve tissue which connects the left and right sides of the brain – has more connections in women than in men, hence our ability to relate better, to connect with emotions more fully and also why we are programmed to keep social harmony. We can participate jointly in decision making with little stress, conflict or the need to display status.

We're faster and more accurate at identifying and controlling emotions. We have 9.5 times as much white matter in our brains than men, which acts like a super highway to connect various parts of the brain to another, which possibly accounts for our ability to all talk at once, listen to myriad conversations and to multi-task. And as you know very well, we navigate through the world very differently!

We're also better at hearing human tonality and sounds than a male and at reading faces. We make more eye contact and react more sympathetically to distress and emotion in others. This is because the *hippocampus* – the hub for emotion and memory formation – is larger in the female brain.

In a nutshell, we have a unique brain circuitry, which is imprinted with ancient instructions on being a woman. Seen under an MRI scan, we use different circuits to a man's brain to accomplish the same goals and tasks. Biology and the way our brain is wired drive our impulses, values and reality, while the gut – also known as the second brain – is the place where we sense and tune in to our intuition. In fact, it appears we're better wired for leadership than men!

Female neurology is like the ocean – calm and serene one moment, stormy and unpredictable the next – as we get swayed by our fluctuating hormones, while a man's neurology is more constant. Most of the month, we are engaged, enthusiastic, productive, intelligent and optimistic – but these hormone fluctuations are very disruptive and we can easily go into self-destruct mode if we're not alert. Before menstruation, we tend to get weepier, more emotionally sensitive, and infuriatingly we don't sleep as much, so tiredness also becomes an issue.

However, for women we also have another place to 'tune in': our womb space, even if it has been surgically removed. This is a place we can sink into and surrender, a place to elicit answers from the deep feminine aspect of ourselves. It has a knowing which the brain doesn't sense and acts more like a second heart. The womb holds the deepest most sacred and ancient secrets of life within every woman.

Now you know the differences (and I've only scraped the surface here) it's important to remember that your mind is a tool – pure and simple. You can use it when necessary and let it rest when not. You are not your brain – you are the *user* of your brain, the Thinker behind your thoughts. Your mind doesn't have to be permanently switched on in hyper-alert mode. And when you no longer identify with your emotions and get swept away by them, but instead observe and learn from them, you are one step closer to being your authentic self.

Chapter 8

Why Thinking Your Way to the Top Just Isn't Enough!

If you want to be brilliant as a leader, you need to be unruffled and at ease on many levels: with your physiology, emotions, feelings, thinking, behaviour, performance and presence. Interestingly, this is where deep hypnosis can be so effective as it dips under the radar of the logical cortex (the thinking part of the brain) to allay all objections, while employing your unconscious (or subconscious mind) to align with the outcomes you so desire.

What's driving your behaviour is the way you think – it determines what to do, which is why the exercises later on in the chapter *Becoming The Mistress of Your Mind* are so powerful as an accompaniment to the other work in this book. Your thoughts, emotions, feelings, behaviours, choices, actions, and so on, are all dictated by your 'autopilot', and despite what you may think or like to believe, you are actually being ruled by your unconscious mind. If you think that for the majority of your waking hours you are actually in cognitive control, think again! Latest Neuro-science research tells us that the input from your conscious mind is restricted to a maximum of 5%. So for a massive 95% of the time, you are running off your unconscious autopilot – all the beliefs and behaviours that you have been taught to believe are true, even if they're not!

Your unconscious mind will take action to fulfil whatever is uppermost in your mind, whether it be good or bad, true or false, in your best interests or not. It just wants to do your bidding – like the Genie in Aladdin's lamp. So once you can let go of the fear, prejudice, arguments, justifications, objections and reasons why you shouldn't live an extraordinary life, and give yourself permission to become an extraordinary leader in your field, it can joyfully help you to be all you can and unleash that potential. At long last!

This therefore also applies to your beliefs. So if you really believe at a conscious level that you can be successful at something, that represents only 5% of your mind power. If what's in your autopilot doesn't agree with you, you're in big trouble, because now you're up against the remaining 95% of your mind that is telling you that you won't be able to achieve it! So no wonder you cannot get to the top with just willpower alone.

Belief, therefore, requires both your conscious and unconscious minds to be congruent and completely aligned with what it is you want to achieve.

However, what you think is also influenced by what you feel. If you're feeling low, you can think yourself into a funk and spend your whole day being non-productive and semi-paralysed. This thinking/feeling goes back and forwards, but the main driver is the way you are *feeling*.

So, if you want to change the way you're thinking right now, you have to change the way you are feeling. If you're feeling anxious, there's no point in someone saying to you, "Don't worry." That's just not enough and does nothing whatsoever to alleviate the anxiety. Even someone pouring praise on your shoulders for your achievements won't hit the spot until *you feel* at the very core of your being – in that 'knowing' inside of you – that you're successful or abundant or healthy or good at what you do. Reasoning alone simply doesn't work. You've got to change how you feel, along with your thinking.

The quality of your thoughts is hugely influenced by your physiology, and your physiology hugely affects your thinking – your psychology. There is no division between your body and your mind.

Have you heard the expression, "Thoughts become things?" Please forgive a gross simplification here, but are you aware that it takes less than 17 seconds for a thought to be transformed – through a series of chemical and electrical interactions – to create a pathway in your neurology? When you keep repeating that same thought, whether good or bad, the energetic and emotional vibration of that thought rushes down the same neural pathway, which eventually turns into the equivalent of a super-highway.

So if your thoughts are those of unworthiness, unhappiness, lack of ability, low self-esteem, overwhelm, or any other thoughts which are keeping you stuck, can you see how easily these can become embedded into your system? And then your life leads out from these deeply embedded thoughts.

It's not always easy to change your thinking if you get caught on the sorry-go-round of misery, so the easiest and fastest way to shift is to change your physiology, rather than the more challenging way of trying to snap out of it, or to think of the poor people suffering in other countries, or how worse things can happen at sea!

Your thoughts, beliefs, attitudes, traumas and life experiences directly influence your biology – in fact, literally shape your brain. We now understand that 75-90% of all illnesses are either caused by or worsened by stress. What you think can influence how sick or well you are. Your mind influences your body – but your body also directly and powerfully influences your brain.

Have you ever felt stressed and anxious and then taken a walk through the woods or on the beach, or ridden your bike a few miles, only to feel calm and relaxed afterwards? Why did it happen? Because you burned off the stress chemicals, adrenaline and cortisol which made you feel anxious.

Have you also ever felt angry and irritable because you've been deprived of sleep, and then felt happier and with fewer problems after a good night's sleep?

Let me give you an example of how your thinking affects your physiology – in other words, your body chemistry. I want you to imagine I've whisked you away to the warm sunny Mediterranean, basking under an azure sky with not a puff of cloud anywhere. On the whisper of a gentle breeze comes the refreshing, pungent, yet sweet, heady aroma of citrus blossom, enticing you to breathe it more deeply into your lungs. So you allow your primordial sense of smell to draw you closer and closer to the origin of the scent. You hear the humming of bees as they go about their business, flitting from flower to flower, supping the nectar, until you reach a lemon grove emitting a glorious citrus perfume.

Rich green leaves and the juiciest fat lemons within arm's reach await your delight, both blossom and fruit on the trees at the same time. And in the warmth of the sun as it caresses your bare arms, you reach out and with a little twist of your wrist, pull off a lemon which comes away easily and effortlessly into your hand. Now, by chance, you happen to have a small fruit knife in your bag. So, resting the lemon carefully on a warm rock, you start to cut the lemon in half. Juice flows out, stinging your fingers and the air is immediately filled with the fresh smell of the zest. Now I want you to put the piece of lemon into your mouth and bite it, letting the juice dribble into your mouth – oohhhh!!

Now, I don't know about you, but I was 'got' about five seconds ago, at the scent wafting through the air, and by the time I was biting the lemon in my imagination, quite frankly, I was dribbling! By now if your nose hasn't wrinkled, your tongue tingled and your mouth watered, then you are a hopeless case!

But I'm only telling you a story. This shows how acutely connected your thoughts are with your body chemistry – and how your imagination can affect what is going on in your body with amazing rapidity.

However, this story wouldn't have any impact if you hadn't already had the experience of the taste and smell of lemon. Similarly, I could wax lyrical about the sounds of waves crashing on the shore and the wetness of salt spray on your face as the splash hits the sea wall, or the rumbling sound of the waves as they gather up the pebbles on the beach and roll them around, sucking them into their power, before dashing them once again on to the sand, or the ozone smell of salty seaweed and the slight tang of iodine in your mouth and the depths of the blue waters reflecting the sky, the shimmer of the light sparkling on the surface and the dance of the white horses on the waves as you look out to sea.

But if you've only ever experienced mountains and meadows, or cities and roads, and never experienced the sea, your imagination alone won't be sufficient to conjure up what the sea is like in reality. You have to *experience* it in order to recall something back into your awareness.

What is the relevance of this? Because we've been trained very well to sink to the lowest common denominator of a sense of unworthiness, of lack, of not being good enough – all the things I talked about earlier in the chapter *Feminine Addictions*. So if you don't have sufficient references to what it *feels* like to be successful in your chosen field, or to be a leader, or to have a great sense of self-esteem, to feel confident talking with people, to be able to accept compliments easily, or to marvel at the magnificence of your own body, or to say "No" with authority and "Yes" with great joy, or to feel relaxed and purposeful at the same time, or passionate about something, you need to find some ways of incorporating them into your *experience*.

And by 'incorporate' I literally mean, as the dictionary says: "bringing them into your body, having a bodily form, embodied" into your cellular memory and into your neurology, so these wonderful, positive feelings become second nature. Used in conjunction with your imagination, you will become so much more powerful, more authentic and more vibrantly successful in your chosen field. You will be able to experience the effects of this in the later chapter on *Dancing With The Archetypes* where you will be able to actually experience these positive feelings of success and incorporate them.

Your memory is not just confined to your brain. Your body has the amazing capacity to record your every action in its cells – what we call muscle memory and cellular memory. If it didn't, every morning you would have to re-learn how to put on your make-up or where to put your hands and feet in order to drive your car. You also have the capacity to recall your experiences, good or bad, by going into the filing cabinet of your memory and focusing on any particular event or feeling and bringing them up into conscious awareness. (You'll find out more on how to bring up fantastic memories and overpower the bad ones in the chapter *Becoming the Mistress of Your Mind.*)

Your muscle memory also stores physical and emotional hurts deep down, which is why sometimes when you receive a deep tissue massage, unbidden memories rise to the surface to be acknowledged and healed, and you may shed lots of tears and not know why. Or there may be just one tiny little spot where if someone drops a sweet gentle kiss there, waves of pleasure and delight flood through your body as your body recalls a special relationship.

> *"Everything is energy, and that's all there is to it.*
> *Match the frequency of the reality you want*
> *and you cannot help but get that reality.*
> *It can be no other way."*

Albert Einstein

When you employ your imagination to recall great memories and then bring them into your body through touch, movement, dance and even mime, you're creating new cellular and muscle memory. So you only have to put your body into those same positions for the beneficial behaviours to arrive in your unconscious awareness. You are, therefore, training your unconscious mind (that 95%), to be on your side in more than one dimension, and reinforcing these supportive patterns in your nervous system. Your neurology literally gets rewired, assisted by all the delicious pleasure-inducing hormones.

Your attitude towards what you think is possible determines what you do – your mindset creates the possibilities, dreams the dreams and your body lives them. Your body physically experiences the activity your mind is creating! What the mind conceives, the body achieves, so even just reading these words will cause a change in your chemistry.

Dancing Your Way To The Top is a far more effortless and fun way of bringing these benefits into your life than having to work it all out! It's the mind/body/spirit combination that makes it so powerful.

Chapter 9
Unveiling the Masks

Can you remember a time when you were little and played at dressing up? Lips daubed with stolen lipstick, cheeks patted with powder puffs, wearing your mother's shoes, staggering around the room and trying not to fall?

Or climbing trees in the park like the boys, racing your bike and careering down the hill on roller skates, or covering yourself with flour when you were stirring the cake mixture in the kitchen?

And then there was the fairy wand, which transformed everything from its drab state into a wonderland of sparkles with one swish and a few magic words.

In my imagination I could be whoever I chose to be, with just a few small props – even a cardboard box under the dining table with a wooden spoon to act as oar and a black handkerchief tied across one eye, served as my pirate ship to sail the seven seas in search of adventure. And a tiny tin of polish, a duster and a little apron kept me in housewife mode for hours!

When my children were small, I made sure we had a large box of dressing-up clothes so they could use their active imaginations and create stories in their heads to play out in the safe environment at home. It was a familiar sight to see fairies and witches, Batman and vampires, wizards and warriors, knights and princesses, astronauts and animals, Hobbits and ogres flit across the kitchen floor, accompanied by hearty cries and weird noises. And to this day, the hairy feet, the black cloak and the scary masks make an appearance from time to time, creating a rich backdrop for grown-up play at fancy-dress parties.

As a child and a teenager, there were roles I shape-shifted in and out of with ease. When we're very little, as the animal part of our brain is growing, we love pretending to be animals like cats and tigers and monkeys. Then, when more cognitive awareness sets in, we look for role models to imitate to help us deal with different aspects of our lives as we grow up, so we take what we see in the world around us, copy the mannerisms, the words and the body language, in order to create a world in which we can survive.

What roles have you played in your life so far? I've been a photographer, film production assistant, model, secretary, wife, mother, businesswoman, campaigner, gardener, Buddhist leader, TV and radio show host, horticulturist, shoe designer, author, rally-car driver, lover, dance teacher, divorcee, psychotherapist, single mother, dutiful daughter, carer, grandmother, and so much more besides.

As I read through that list, I'm immediately transported back to what I was wearing, the 'uniform' that went with each of these roles and the 'props' that made them fully and instantly recognisable. There's an energy about each one of these roles, a *modus operandi,* a style and a script if you're going to play them properly. In fact, we're playing roles, or wearing 'masks' as I like to think of them, all day long.

"All the world's a stage and all the men and women merely players."

William Shakespeare

Some years ago when I was a single mum, I had a part-time job as a receptionist in a private hospital. This involved me wearing a crisp white uniform. I loved wearing it, as suddenly I felt very professional in my role; it was literally like stepping into another world – not quite like putting Catwoman's suit on, but affording me a similar feeling of authority and protection. Interestingly, the patients treated me like a doctor (what is called 'White–coat Syndrome') and before long, the consultants had upgraded me to look after patients going for MRI scans, counselling and patient care. So can you see the impact of a uniform and a mask? And now there are even dating sites for uniform-wearers!

Then there are the emotional aspects to masks: sad, patient, victim, martyr, bad, good, rebel, depressed, happy, benevolent, successful, failure, innocent, predatory, sexual, caring, dutiful, grieving, loving – and I'm sure you can add to that list.

Masks are a perceptual lens, not just a way of *seeing* the world, but a complete way of *experiencing* the world. We look around and see others in that role and assume that is the way we also have to play it. Masks are also very convenient to hide our light behind!

I remember when I first got married that I felt as a wife I now had to behave in a completely different way, and not only that, dress in a different way that befitted my status. So out of the window went the frivolity, the sexiness and the youthful innocence, and in stepped the sensible, practical, dutiful wife as I looked around at the new crowd we were spending time with, modelling myself on their behaviour, together with how I remembered my mother when I was growing up. Little wonder my ex-husband found his secretaries, with their skirts little more than waistbands and their conveniently unbuttoned blouses with more than a suggestion of flirtatious breasts, somewhat more appealing than me!

Even as grown-ups, women shape-shift with fluidity throughout their day, possibly more so than men whose roles have a greater stability and structure to them. Men seem to have a greater understanding that business is just a game to be played by certain rules.

Just today you may have shape-shifted from lover to mediator to mother to wife to chauffeur to commuter to businesswoman to colleague to manager to boss to victim to leader to friend to confidante to one of the gang and then back again to mother, nurse, cook, wife or myriad roles in between. Sound familiar?

What masks do you hide behind?
Who do you become when you step out on to the stage of life?

I'd like you to make a list of your masks and then begin to notice them as you take one off and put a new one on throughout the day. Start to be playful with these and notice how often you hide away and don't allow your true self to shine through.

When you've done that, I'd like you to think about the reply you give to people when they ask you what you do: e.g. "I'm a manager; I'm just a housewife and mother; I'm a gardener; I'm a midwife; I'm in IT; I'm a dancer; I'm a coach; I'm an artist; I'm a financial advisor; I'm a brain surgeon."

The fact is, you are not your name, your role, your job, the uniform you wear, the mask you hide behind, the country you live in, your religion, your politics.

Now ask yourself: "Who am I really?"

And drop down to the level beneath that.

Keep asking the question "Who am I?" dropping down to the next layer and keep asking until you feel those masks falling away and you begin to tap into the essence of your authentic self.

When tears begin to fall, you know you've got there. It's often a place of peace and calm, or bliss and gentleness, or joy and love. Just sit with this and experience it – give yourself the time and space to just be here with the essence of you.

This is also a lovely exercise to do with a friend who will keep asking the question – "Who are you?" Someone who will be there to witness the change in you, as it doesn't just happen in your head – your essence will suffuse the whole of your being and I assure you will be wonderful to see.

When you're ready now, bring that wonderful feeling back up through the layers until you come back to being the woman with all that awesomeness inside you. This is who you really are at your authentic core.

This is the deepest part of you that knows no bounds, so it also needs to have safe boundaries in place and its vulnerabilities respected. It needs taking care of in this fast-paced world, with all its cares and worries.

I now want to find ways of helping you express this beautiful energy in everything you do.

Why is this important with leadership? Because leadership in the first part of the 21st century requires us to be authentic: to no longer hide behind the masks we once wore.

Chapter 10
Stepping into Your True Identity

In many workshops I've led, I've observed how many women hold their body with rigidity, their shoulders around their ears like chickens, as if they were holding it all together for fear of letting go and falling apart, and essentially shutting off parts of who they really are. And then of course we have the latest must-have underwear – corsets, uplifting bras, body-shaping miracles hidden under our clothes.

If you've ever been in a ladies rest-room as women unburden themselves of these skin-tight torture garments, you'll hear lots of huffing and puffing as they battle with these 21st century chastity belts, and a big sigh of relief when released from their clutches.

Yes, I know they make us look better as they hold all the spare bits tightly in, but when we live like that, as if everything has to be held in, we lose a sense of connection with our real self and our freedom to breathe, while we again succumb to the 'look, but don't touch' scenario, accompanied by the fear of being found out as less than perfect. Even our shoes confine us as we stagger around in high heels. (You try running for safety in a pair of Louboutins!)

Our present lifestyle has also confined us to sitting mostly in chairs, crouched over computers, bent over steering wheels and exercise bikes, or huddled on sofas – a million miles away from the way our bodies were designed. Our ability to communicate has been stifled, despite tremendous advances in technology, as we're now confined to abbreviated versions of true expression, and the ubiquitous text, email or social media post in place of handwritten letters and real face-to-face encounters and live conversations.

In fact, in our pursuit of advancement, we've actually regressed in terms of a richness of external expression and an ability to be fully self-expressed.

Let me ask you a question: do you feel you're different? Have you ever felt that you didn't fit in? No matter where I go, when I ask women these questions, the majority raise their hands. As a result of doing everything in our power to conform, we've rejected and covered up our true impulses and instincts. This is like writing a prescription for burnout! We've shape-shifted to appear different from who we really are, taking ourselves in the process a long way away from a sense of wellbeing and self-belief.

Fear of difference actually is the result of a weak identity. Interestingly, military societies and careers where soldiers can disguise their true identity under a uniform, and are told what to think and what not to think, dehumanise people, which is why they're able to kill on demand. To a certain extent, it's the same with organised religions, politics and corporations, where if you don't toe the party line, you'll be sidelined.

It all boils down to a disqualification of your identity. And we've jumped on the bandwagon of women being classified as second-class citizens.

We've got into the habit of identifying with what is wrong in life: with sickness, with disappointment and with failure. In other words, we've learned to sink to the lowest common denominator in order to fit in.

Does any of this sound familiar? When people ask you how you are, what do you say? "I'm getting there." (Where on earth is "there?") or, "I'm exhausted," as if you earn Brownie points for how tired you are. Or do you play the 'Fake it till you make it' game, as I referred to before, pretending all is going swimmingly yet deep under the water you're paddling furiously to keep afloat, praying that no one will uncover your vulnerability?

When you reconnect with your instincts and strengthen your true identity (as opposed to your personality), something shifts inside, which leads you towards a deeper respect for all forms of life – including your own! When your identity is well defined and healthy, your limits are very clear as well and you're able to give clear feedback to those around you.

When you step into your own essence, go deep inside to awaken your tenderness, vulnerability, compassion and joy, and fully express those feelings which you've denied for so long, you'll stop feeding that negative side of your ego which insists on suffering. This is about nurturing a healthy identity where all the parts of you that were disparate now become integrated; where you nurture your vitality, your ability to connect with others, your healthy sexuality, your creativity and your heart-centred sense of being.

When you relax deeply and go inside, you have access to a new state of consciousness, where you may even expand towards cosmic awareness. If you read the autobiographies of many famous inventors and artists, this is where they go to for inspiration – they move beyond the strictures and limitations of their imposed external identity in order to discover a different perception of reality, where their own identity also becomes stronger. Your identity is related to your self-esteem, your own self-value and personal values, so it overflows like a fountain of pleasure.

"Your vision will only become clear when you look into your heart.
Who looks outside, dreams.
Who looks inside, awakens."

Carl Gustav Jung

What's really important to you in life? What are *your* values that you live by? Knowing your values is one of the most important things you can do. Your values are the way you choose to live your life, what you consider to be your highest priorities at this particular moment in time – and they may well evolve as you move through life. Each decade tends to bring a new shift in our values.

Whatever value is highest will spontaneously inspire you from within – no motivation needed, as you want to express that intrinsic value in your life. Your highest values are where you are empowered – your lowest often leave you drained and uninspired. In fact, your life demonstrates your values.

Each person's values are unique to them, like a fingerprint. No two people have the same values in exactly the same order – what is called the 'hierarchy of values'. It is your value system that determines your destiny, how you perceive the world and how you act in it.

The tendency is for us to project our own values on to other people. We notice all the differences (while remaining blind to our similarities), and punish others for not being like us. You can't expect someone else to live up to your values and fantasies, or you'll always set yourself up for failure. It so happens we all live according to our own values – not anyone else's. You have to be true to who you are and allow other people to be true to themselves too. The fact is, every value and attribute is neutral until someone has an opinion about it and judges it.

Some people think that you have to have the same values as your partner in order to have a satisfying and fulfilling life, but what if that weren't so? What if, by sharing identical values, your relationship can become dull and boring and stilted? If you and your partner are identical, one of you doesn't need to be there! However, it's very important that your values are linked and aligned, rather than conflicting. And this goes for business relationships, too.

When you find out exactly what your own values are, it becomes so much easier for you to make decisions and steer the course of your life. When you answer the questions below, you'll discover what's truly important to you in life, and thereby where your values lie.

- *How do you fill the space you are living in, your environment?*

  You'll fill it according to what is special to you – e.g. books, flowers, antiques, cups and trophies, family portraits, sports memorabilia…

- *Where do you focus your energy most?*

  There will be things you love to do which you'll always find the time and energy to focus on, no matter how tired you are – they become a priority in your life over anything else.

- *What do you spend your money on?*

  Where the majority of your money goes is a clear indication of what you consider to be most important. Is it on children, your home, clothes, food, health and fitness, a pension scheme, adventure, entertainment, travel, technology, education, personal growth, spiritual development, gardening, sports, charity?

- *What do you pay attention to?*

  If there's something on the news or on television or a conversation, what grabs your attention? Is it to do with finance, sport, health, music, nature, history?

- *What goes on in your head?*

  What do you think and daydream about?

- *What would you love to do if time and money were not an issue?*

  What's your heart's desire?

Other people will have different values with a different order of priority, but you won't experience a profound connection in relationships with others unless you understand and respect *their* values.

How do you find out what someone else's values are? Pay attention to what they talk about, what they do, how they live and how they spend their money. It will be exactly according to their personal hierarchy of values, so you can then choose whether or not you can live with that.

Wisdom is honouring other peoples' value systems, and knowing they're going to live by them anyway, regardless of how much we try to change them – and knowing it's futile to try! So it's at this point that your feminine wisdom needs to step in and determine *who* you're going to associate with – whose values align with yours.

Living *up* to your own values rather than living *down* to somebody else's is vital on the path to Leadership, where you go out into the world, proudly and joyfully, with head held high – walking your own talk.

Chapter 11
The Influencing Model

I've already mentioned the 'Fake it till you make it' strategy often advised to help you reach the higher echelons of leadership. How has that worked for you so far?

We've talked about 'masks' and 'uniforms' and the behaviours that accompany them. But the trouble is, anyone with a pulse can tell when you're faking it, unless you're a consummate actress!

Besides which, faking it leads you inexorably towards 'The Imposter Syndrome' with its accompanying fear of being found out, which inevitably goes on to feed a lack of self-esteem, and self-criticism and defensiveness. And so the downward spiral continues...

In my travels I've come across many courses and books about body language and how we need to learn to engage with our eyes, where to put our hands in order to be seen as confident, what to do and what not to do in order to be taken seriously and to be able to influence others. So, is body language that important? In short, yes, but I'm talking about it here in a different way, one which doesn't involve strategies. Your expressions, hand gestures and facial expressions are non-verbal communications at a subconscious level and are the indicators of your true feelings and intentions.

You'll notice this especially in the political or media arena where body language can make or break a speaker or celebrity before they've even started to talk. (In fact, in some cases, their body language is so at odds with what they're actually saying, it becomes clear that they can't be trusted!) You need to be congruent with your message – if *you* don't believe what you are saying, your body language will betray you. You cannot force your body to act as though you believe something!

Feminine Leadership is all about developing your authentic body language to convey your true strength, confidence and presence as a leader rather than insecurity and uncertainty – but remember this is an inside job, something to be *drawn out from within*, not something to be imposed from the outside.

Somehow in our journey towards profit we've forgotten about being genuine and trustworthy which are also keys to new leadership. When we're being our authentic selves, there's no need for ego. Unfortunately, business training up until now has been all about the image we present to the world. It's time to change that and allow ourselves to be dynamically, crazily, juicily who we really are! Otherwise we get entrapped within a bland normality and mediocrity that has no energy and innovation about it. And what the world needs right now is energetic and innovative female leaders!

Here I want to show you how you can claim and own the magnificence of your authentic self, without comparing yourself with anyone else. When you are being fully you, you won't be thinking about how you appear to others. You will be far too busy just 'Being'.

It's highly stressful to be self-consciously focusing on what others think of you, accompanied by a gigantic knock to your self-esteem when you feel you don't match up. Love you or hate you, when you're being authentic, people will respect and honour that and either follow you or not. Their choice!

When we look at highly successful people who are leaders in their own field, they don't care what others think of them. They're just focused on making a difference. When you try to twist yourself into the shape of a pretzel to fit in, that is when you lose credibility. And it's worth noting at this juncture that not everyone *is* going to love you – as the saying goes: "You can please some of the people some of the time, but not all the people all of the time." So please, get over yourself!

What if you were to stop faking it and actually claim and own all the attributes you already have to take you to the top of your game?

Do you know that the way you hold your body and use it says much more about you than anything else? It's the first thing other people notice before you even open your mouth, and it's within those first vital seconds of meeting that someone will size you up, and make decisions and judgements about you. In fact, it's said that you have less than three seconds to make a first impression. There's an energy that emanates from you that you can't hide, which acts like an advert! Your presence when you walk into a room has the ability to lighten it up or darken it down.

So how would it be if you could enhance your presence from where it is now to radiate even more love and light and strength and compassion and joy and natural leadership?

There's a direct correlation between your physicality and what's going on inside your head – your thoughts, feelings, emotions and deep-seated beliefs. You unconsciously reveal whether you're happy or sad, depressed or angry, spiritually tuned-in or lacking connection, confident or beset with low self-esteem, stressed or relaxed, whether you feel loved or are defensive, and even whether you're sexually fulfilled. It also shows whether your diet is good or bad. You see, the body never lies! And no amount of body-language training will fool people if everything else is not congruent and in alignment.

"Your biography becomes your biology!"

Dr. Candace Pert – Molecules of Emotion

Your vitality, sexuality, creativity, your caring attitude and your connection with other people radiate from you and are on show all the time. The story of your life, in other words your biography, literally becomes your biology! And with the advent of video in all its forms, whether through public media sites or private video calls, you're now more transparent and observable than ever before.

Your emotions and the way you use your body are inextricably linked. The way you move affects the way you think, feel and behave, and conversely the way you feel also affects the way your body expresses itself. Everything from walking, clapping and jumping to frowning, smiling, laughter and tears, to the smallest movements in the muscles of the face, affects your body chemistry. To put it another way, emotion is created by motion. Emotion from a scientific perspective is an energy-electron in motion.

So can you imagine how much you can affect the way you show up by changing the way you feel about life and your body, and how you can affect your emotions by the way you move? When you start to change your body language, you give your confidence a huge boost. I like to call it: 'Emotional Keep-Fit'.

Your physiology radically affects your mental state and the way you think, feel and behave. By letting go of limitations, programming and mindsets that hold you back, your new awareness will support you in making good decisions – the right decisions. Certain movements help you reveal your genius, promote greater self-esteem and confidence and also contribute towards you expressing yourself more courageously, so you shine with a presence and radiance that is naturally successful. And very attractive to others!

Your body language, physicality and physiology affect *everything* – the way you feel, your emotions, your energy, your mood, the way others perceive and 'read' you, your ability to understand feedback at a non-verbal level and also how you communicate. They affect your mindset, your sexual and energetic life force, your productivity and your success in business.

When you incorporate (literally bring into your body's awareness and cellular memory) feelings of success, imprint them on to your unconscious mind, and learn to trust your intuition, your ability to rise to the top and stay there will be unstoppable.

The exercises in *Dance Your Way To The Top!* are geared towards enriching your self-esteem, self-confidence, and having better relationships, enhanced communication skills, flexibility and progression in your business. They will help you to move, think and use even your verbal language in a more empowering way, inspiring vitality, creativity and unleashing your potential for living a more productive life, all of which have a profound knock-on effect on your mental and physical health.

My 'Influencing Model' opposite shows how very important your physiology and physicality is in influencing not only others around you, but also your own mind. Until very recently, it was said that your physiology accounts for a massive 55%, what you focus on 38%, and the words you use 7%. Those statistics have now been debunked by Albert Mehrabia, the professor behind the original study, but your physiology and your life-force does indeed have a major impact, in fact the greatest impact until you open your mouth – then the tonality and intensity of your voice, your intention and your choice of words start to work in conjunction with your body language.

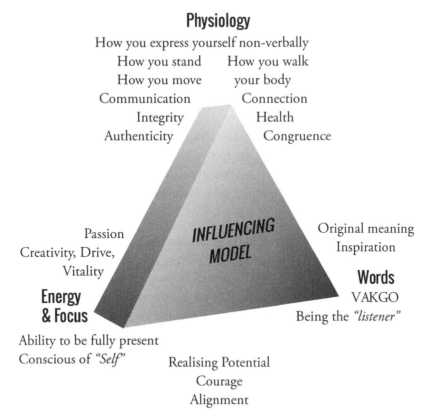

Physiology
How you express yourself non-verbally
How you stand How you walk
How you move your body
Communication Connection
Integrity Health
Authenticity Congruence

INFLUENCING
MODEL

Passion Original meaning
Creativity, Drive, Inspiration
Vitality
Words
Energy VAKGO
& Focus Being the *"listener"*

Ability to be fully present
Conscious of *"Self"*
Realising Potential
Courage
Alignment
Dependent Upon: Values and Beliefs

Susie Heath © 2012

Whether you realise this or not, your ability to influence as a leader will ultimately supersede your talent, ability, education, knowledge, experience or any other quality that you bring to the table.

"Influence – the capacity or power of persons or things to be a compelling force on, or produce effects on the actions, behaviour or opinions of others."

as defined by the English dictionary

We think that the words we use are the most important factor when it comes to influencing and leading others, but in fact they only account for a small percentage; so when you focus all your attention on rehearsing that all-important speech or rewriting and re-hashing your presentation to within an inch of its life, you may be placing your focus in the wrong area.

Indeed, it's not so much *what* you say and do that people remember, but *how you leave them feeling*. And this is vital information for you as a leader.

**Most important of all is that your body language
is in alignment with what you say.
Authenticity is key!**

Feminine Leadership also embraces 'being the listener' – in other words, listening with an open heart, an open mind and with total awareness, not only to what the other is saying, without prejudice, judgement, comparison or criticism (all masculine traits), but also to what *you* are saying, both to yourself inside your head, and out loud.

It's vital too that we look to the original meaning of the words we use. In fact, if you look at a dictionary pre-1945, that is what your body responds to. The vibration and original meaning of words are embedded in your DNA from the ancestral energy of your parents and grandparents. This is particularly pertinent when we think of the way language is used by young people today when they say 'sick' meaning 'good' and 'bad' meaning 'good'. Their body will respond after time to the original meaning!

Words fascinate me: the world 'hearth' has the word 'heart' in it. 'Earth' is 'heart' just with the letters in a different order. So also with 'silent' and 'listen.' 'Evil' is 'live' spelled backwards – in other words anti-life! There are many more examples in the English language, and I've heard that in other languages too such similarities occur.

People's perception of the world differs depending on which modality is most in the forefront of the way they personally assimilate language – whether it is Visual (seeing), Auditory (hearing), Kinaesthetic (feeling), Gustatory (taste), or Olfactory (smell) – hence V-A-K-G-O on my diagram. There is also Digital to add to that list for people (more men than women here), who assimilate the world around them in a more technical and logical way. When we communicate as leaders, therefore, when we include all these modalities, everyone feels at some level as if we're talking to, and including them.

Your focus and energy also accounts for a massive percentage. You will no doubt have heard that whatever you focus your attention on expands – so you will get more of what you are thinking about, whether that is good or bad. So if you want to be a great leader, healthy, happy, joyful, aware, skilful, abundant, successful, appreciated, listened to, wise, and so on, place your attention on those aspects – not on the lack of them! You'll be intrigued how this alone can alter the course of your life.

Energy includes not only your physical energy, but also your emotional energy, your spiritual energy, your sexual energy, and much more besides. Energy includes your connection to All That Is, The Divine, the Universe, God, your Higher Self, or however you refer to that Power that is greater than you. The vibration of your verbal expression – the energy of the words you use, the tonality of your voice, as well as the timbre and volume in your vocal delivery, also influences it.

Presence, we've noted before, is also one of the most important attributes of a leader. What is it about those singers, actors and orators who stir us at such a deep level? We know it's not just their words. It's their *presence* – they literally fill the stage to the extent that we can't take our eyes off them, as we hang on their every word, even if we can't remember a single thing they actually said afterwards!

We can literally feel a pull of energy as we sense a strong desire to be nearer to them, as we lean towards them, while those we don't like will repel us as they push their energy at us. Used with integrity, this is a wonderful tool for leadership, but as history has shown, it can also be used by manipulative and evil people for horrifying deeds.

Conscious of Self as opposed to being self-conscious is where we're aware of the difference we can make to others, rather than worrying about what others think of our performance and us. This state of consciousness is what we are aiming for.

The exercises in *Dance Your Way To The Top!* are designed to be a journey in which you unleash your true authenticity, so you can be a leader of influence, of integrity and inspiration. The depth that this takes you to has the potential to transform every interaction, so you don't have to strive to change anything. It will all come to you naturally because you are '*Being*'. It's a question of un-learning what is not you and allowing your true, magnificent self to shine through.

"Example is not the main thing in influencing others; it is the only thing."

Albert Schweitzer

Emotional intelligence, more of a feminine trait, is now valued as highly as IQ. Businesses have woken up to the value of highly developed emotional intelligence as the bottom line is it *affects* the bottom line! It's these 'extra' qualities – intuition, empathy, compassion, responsibility and people skills – that set so many female leaders apart and are a tremendous asset to enterprises.

What follows may fly in the face of what you've previously been taught about leadership, but please stay with me. I learned the hard way, by making the oh-so-foolish assumption that men were far better equipped to teach me all about business and success and public speaking than women!

As a result, I learned to make power moves with my hands and body, to be strident and dominating, to wear my 'uniform' where everything had to be perfect, to be assertive and authoritative and to not show vulnerability. But in time, this masculinised behaviour (where I failed to listen to my true nature, my body and my intuition), led me down the hard road of burnout.

In fact, the only time I was my true self on stage was when I was lecturing for The Royal Horticulture Society in London, when I went into another mode of connection with nature due to my sheer joy in talking about plants, their origins and how to grow them. Somehow, I made it acceptable in the horticultural world to sashay across the stage like a plant in the breeze, or to mimic the movements of an insect in the jungle!

From my dance training and from my work with masculine and feminine dynamics, I've learned that outbursts of masculine energy where we are decisive, active and outward, logical, powerful and focused and in achievement mode where we use our conscious, energetic sympathetic nervous system, need to be tempered with the soft, gentle, intuitive, inward and emotionally intelligent parasympathetic system – the two energies functioning like a wave in flow, rather than an either/or situation.

This is vital for restoration of our bodily functions, rejuvenation and relaxation from stress. In fact as a woman, the ideal for us – in order to operate at optimum levels for health of both body and mind and to avoid burnout – is to be using approximately 70% of our feminine energies of tenderness, compassion, connection, cooperation, intuition and nurturing, and only around 30% of masculine energy, remembering that that is our emergency reserve, a borrowed, learnt response.

Our feminine energy includes elements of fluidity, gracefulness, elegance, sensuality, expressive gestures, relaxed shoulders and curved, gentle and free-flowing movements, as well as a softer, more expressive voice.

It's always about the way in which you *own* your body, and own the space in which you stand. It's about your radiance, your smile, your connection and your presence. If that sounds fluffy and weak, just think about the way women like Meryl Streep, Oprah, Judi Dench, Michelle Obama, Helen Mirren and countless others like them light up the room: it's not through a strident voice, arrogance or aggressive behaviour. They counterbalance their masculine and feminine energies perfectly.

Your power to influence will enable you to get your message across to more people and help them... because they'll trust what you have to say. And once people trust you, they'll listen to you.

Persuasion and influence are not the same thing. Persuasion is when you use a set of tactics to gain compliance from someone or get them to do what you want them to. Influence is a state of your identity. It's your unique presence. It's who you are.

Feminine Leadership also requires awareness, flexibility, fluidity, a willingness to go with the flow and to adapt at a moment's notice. You can't step into Feminine Leadership if you have no basic trust in life or yourself, so the exercises in the chapters that follow will bring that sense of trust into your awareness.

Knowing how to be a good leader can separate you from the 'ordinary' majority and help you to achieve success and prosperity for your business, as well as that all-important balance for you as a woman.

Leadership comes from within, and is about sensitivity, communicating well, leading by example, and being the one that others look up to, by the potency of our presence and the communication of our vision.

Chapter 12
Feminine Core Energy Dynamics

If you've been sold on the idea of work/life balance, then come closer, as I want to whisper a secret in your ear. Personally, I think work/life balance is a fallacy, a load of bunkum, an unattainable myth that still keeps us feeling 'less than'. There is no such thing in this technological age. Balance actually suggests a cessation of movement where there is no agitation, where everything is still and at peace. All very well, but what about the light and shade of life, the highs and the lows, the colour and variety, the vibrancy and vitality of being alive?

Even if you're on a tightrope over Niagara Falls balancing and holding that state of equilibrium, the only way to move forwards is to take one foot off the only thing that's keeping you stable, a state which no doubt you'll recognise as being very wobbly and precarious indeed!

So instead of work/life balance, I like to call it 'Energy Dynamics' where everything shifts and changes, where you adapt and flow, adjust and fine-tune to create more harmony. The dictionary definition for 'dynamic' is: 'characterised by force of personality, ambition, energy, new ideas'. Now doesn't that sound much more interesting? It's an invitation to a dance – working with rhythm and harmony, fast and slow, backwards and forwards, leading and following, giving and receiving, flowing and moving around obstacles; progress and regress, movement and stillness, taking by the hand and being taken by the hand, surrendering to the music and movement of life.

So with that lovely visual in mind, my premise is that you're not broken – you don't need 'mending', despite what might be going on in your life right now. Instead, I'd like to help you dissolve what isn't authentically you, to leave it all behind, and reveal what *is* you – the you that you were aware of when you were very little, but didn't know how to express or how to connect with as a grown-up. Truly great leaders are authentically tuned in to themselves, so that they can, in turn, authentically tune in to others.

As little children you looked to your caregivers to teach you about the world and how to interact with it. However, unfailingly, what you were taught were *their* limiting self-beliefs, *their* own mind-programming which had been foisted on them throughout their lives, together with society's conditioning and programmes from religion and the media.

Parents will do everything they can to pass on their own beliefs, whether these are good and nourishing or harmful and detrimental – all generally done with the best of intentions to keep their children safe. No doubt you too will do so to your own children if you have them, but hopefully, after reading this book and others on consciousness, you will be so much more aware. My premise though, is that you know deep inside who you are – my job is to jolt your memory, to remind you!

When I was nursing my father during the last few weeks of his life, he kept asking for reassurance that he'd lived a good life. His regrets were of not being able to paint another picture, and of not being around to see his great-grandchildren grow up. He wanted to know that he had lived well, loved well and that he could die in peace with himself. He also was amazed that I was looking after him, and wanted to acknowledge me and who I'd become, something he hadn't done much of when he was well.

The strict authoritarian man, whom I'd been slightly afraid of, suddenly became warm, loving and caring and full of emotions that he shared with me. I'd had glimpses of this deep, vulnerable soul over the years, but when they'd become visible, he'd so often shut them away again. I was so sad that we hadn't had years of this together, but just three short, intense weeks instead. However, in those last few days, we became closer than we'd ever been – it was a beautiful healing time for both of us: peaceful, joyful and loving, yet tinged with sadness at the inevitable approaching end. For the first time, he revealed the true vulnerable man behind the often harsh, critical front he'd presented to me in the past.

Why am I telling you this? Because I want you to be able to get to the end of your life knowing that you've played full-out, been true to who you really are, lived your life the way you chose, instead of dancing to someone else's tune, and having inspired others to do the same. In other words, stepping into your own leadership.

In that very last breath, you won't be saying: "I wish I'd spent more time on social media platforms, watched the news more often, worked harder at the office or had a facelift." You'll want to know that there are no regrets, that you've made your peace with everyone around you, that you've made a difference, put a mark on the world as you've moved through it, that there's nothing or no one to forgive or be forgiven by, that there is no fear, no anger, no regret, no guilt. No thoughts of: "Hold on – I haven't had a chance to be the real me yet!"

> *"Life should not be a journey to the grave with the intention of arriving safely in a pretty and well-preserved body, but rather to skid in broadside in a cloud of smoke, thoroughly used-up, totally worn-out, and loudly proclaiming, 'Wow! What a ride!'"*

Hunter S. Thompson

How about daring to live life *your* way with all your magnificence and faults and mistakes and crazy ideas and creativity and uniqueness? And if you're not any of these, you're missing out – so take off that mental corset that restricts you and holds you in and be prepared to let go and release who you really are deep inside. You'll be amazed at how extraordinary she is and the difference she's going to make to the world! Life is precarious and can be snuffed out like a candle at any moment, so every single minute is infinitely precious!

A few words here about that word which, in my opinion, is overused and subversive, rather than helpful for us as women: *Potential.*

The dictionary defines 'potential' as:

> *'Possible, as opposed to actual. Capable of being or becoming. A latent excellence or ability that may or may not be developed.'*

Now I don't know about you, but I've had enough of 'potential' and being kept in our place, with still a long, long way to go. In fact, it's my belief that the very word 'potential' has kept women in particular from rising to the top in leadership roles, both in our own minds as well as in the external world.

The antonym of potential is described thus:

> *'Real, substantiated, authentic, genuine, bona-fide, true, actual, established, existent, demonstrated, factual, confirmed, authenticated, effective, proven.'*

Can you feel the shift in energy and power of that? This is where I choose to be! I'm not going to wait till I 'grow up', and so I invite you to also put aside your 'potential' and start to actualise!! And by doing so, you also empower others to do the same.

Now at first glance, this may sound acutely selfish, because no doubt, like most girls, you were taught to put yourself at the bottom of the pile. However, probably the most selfish thing you can do in your life is to look to your own needs last, to *not* share the brilliance of who you really are with the world, to *not* take care of yourself and fulfil your purpose on this planet.

We only have a limited amount of energy. It doesn't matter how young you are, how positive you are or how big your goals and dreams. If you don't have the energy moment by moment to support them, you're not going to get to where you want to be.

Grounded in the convergence of the teachings of ancient wisdom, alongside the basic principles of quantum physics, I'm going to share with you how to partner with the Universal Laws of Life to create a transformation by engaging your intuition, and making choice and opportunity your habitual approach to life, rather than the repetitive patterns of old behaviours – to help you identify and claim the gifts you're here to share, to step fully into them and to support others to do the same.

As you begin to tap into the greatest version of yourself, you'll become a role model for your family, your community, your company, your country and even the world. You'll have the courage to act on your core energy – who you really are – for the greater good of all, but by putting yourself first. And, if at this point you're thinking again how selfish it is to put yourself first, may I remind you of the airplane analogy of putting on your own oxygen mask first, before going to the rescue of others?

Because if you don't look after yourself first, you become a burden; other people have to fill in for you, and you miss out, big time.

Following you will find the Feminine Core Energy Dynamics Wheel™, to help you ascertain, from your own point of view, exactly where you

106

are *being true to yourself*, how far you have strayed from being your authentic self, and where you can choose to start making dramatic changes. This is a great exercise to do at least four times a year at the beginning of each season. By the time you reach the end of this book, your scores will have altered dramatically as you integrate more and more of the understanding here into your body and into your life.

Imagine those inner circles to be graduating towards a rich golden centre. This is like taking a slice through your inner core, like the rings of a tree trunk, to find out what is really going on and how close you are being to that core energy that is *the real you*, that golden core where you feel in your own skin, where all feels right with the world no matter what is going on around you, where you know you are living at your optimum in your own way.

Before you start, I want to remind you, you are as unique as a snowflake. You were not born to be like someone else. You were born to be *you* – the best you, you could be. And if you're not there yet, that's fine – you haven't been taught that being you is OK. You haven't been taught that being you is the most precious thing. You haven't been taught that your whole purpose in life is to *bring who you are* to the planet in whatever shape or form that is.

Without any judgement, just mark on each segment where you feel your life is at this moment in time – not against any perceived score, but where you actually are, right here right now, with 0 being low down on the scale and 10 being totally fulfilled.

The closer you are to the centre, the closer you are to your authentic self. But please be gentle on yourself here; there is no failure! Now add up the scores and take that number away from 100. The resultant score is the amount of 'you' you have yet to unlock and discover, the amount you have to play with. So you may find you have only been living a small percentage of your life up till now.

It takes energy and effort to hold on to what is *not* you. So I want again to help you remember who you really are deep inside, because that is what will move mountains at this point in time.

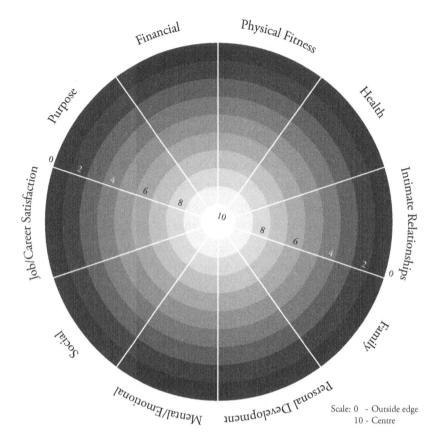

Now come with me to see what we can do to make those scores even higher as you journey closer to that golden centre.

Chapter 13

Why Dance Your Way to the Top?

Many scientific studies have been done on the effects of dance and movement. It's been found to promote mental and emotional health, inspiration and self-expression, and to balance the body's hormones, leaving you feeling energised and creative, and with enhanced self-esteem. It removes stress, overwhelm, misery, depression and loneliness, as well as a feeling of being stuck.

Doesn't that sound like a better recipe than sitting at your desk, head in hand, trying to work it all out?

Your stress and relaxation response is controlled by your brain's command and control centre, called the hypothalamus. Whenever there's a drama or emergency (however you may perceive it at the time), the stress response switches on which sends messages to every part of your body through the automatic part of your nervous system called the sympathetic nervous system. When this is switched on (which it is for most of us most of the time in the 21st century!) your adrenal glands release more cortisol, and the neurotransmitters adrenaline and noradrenaline are produced which are stimulating and energising – all very useful in a dire emergency.

However, so much of life is perceived as an emergency nowadays – from receiving a phone bill that is higher than expected, or that rush of adrenalin in the pit of your stomach when you hear a police car siren even if you're driving at the correct speed!

For our cavewomen ancestors, the stress response would be switched on with a huge jolt only if there was a potential threat to which she had to fight, play dead or run away. It was then switched off immediately the danger was passed, just like animals in the wild, and she would shake out the stress for a few minutes with no harm done to her system.

The problem in our culture is the relentless, chronic, unremitting stress and endless, continual, demanding inputs to our nervous system – even the bleep of a text or an email coming in acts like an alarm system that we feel we need to respond to with urgency, let alone the sound of traffic or fire engine sirens blaring, or TV adverts or the news.

When I was a child, if you phoned someone and they weren't there, that's just how it was, so you tried again another time. No answer machine, no cell phones, no SMS, no email, no Skype, no instant anything. When a telegram arrived, you would probably respond straight away, but business was conducted by post – snail-mail – where you had a few days to mull over a response, or face to face or by telephone or over business lunches.

Nowadays, on top of the hurry-worry instant access world we live in, we have nutrient-deprived foods, toxic environments, electro/techno-pollution and loss of a sense of control, family and community as many people sit, lonely, in front of their computer thinking that they're communicating, when really they're just connecting at a superficial level.

It's amazing *any* of us are standing upright, as all this stress puts us in a state of chronic alarm, leading to overactivation of the sympathetic nervous system and stress response, leading to burnout.

Your body governs your stress and relaxation responses through your autonomic nervous system, which controls all of the automatic functions in your body. This system is divided into two parts: the sympathetic nervous system which you don't have control over (such as your heartbeat and your blood flow) and the parasympathetic nervous system, which is partially automated, but which also responds to your thoughts, feelings and emotions.

So while stress is controlled by your sympathetic nervous system, you have control over the inputs that cause stress, but no control over the response itself. If you perceive stress, your body will react. Relaxation is the best thing you can do to counteract this – but just be aware that you can be relaxed with apathy, boredom, detachment, negativity and indifference or relaxed and positive with equanimity, contentment and curiosity.

Most of us have no clue that sitting around on our sofa watching TV damages our brain. Within seconds, it puts us into a highly suggestible hypnotic state which provides easy access to our subconscious mind where it can alter existing beliefs and form new ones, making it easy for advertisers to influence us without us even being aware of it, as we move from the logical left side of the brain to the more creative right side. It's easy to become addicted to television as it causes the body to release those natural sedatives called endorphins, so it can then reprogramme our minds! I wonder if that is why they're called 'programmes'?

Losing a few hours sleep affects us chemically and hormonally; drinking a sugary fizzy drink, a large coffee or two glasses of wine, talking on our mobile phones for an hour or having an argument all affect our body chemistry and can contribute to burnout in the long term.

Walking, short bursts of lifting weights (which helps sculpt your muscles and is in fact really good for us as women if not taken to excess), and just dancing around, release growth and rejuvenation hormones. *Just please be aware that very heavy or prolonged endurance – 'masculinised' forms of exercise, will deplete your energy and alter your female hormones.*

Your memory and mood centre in the brain, the *hippocampus*, is most sensitive to this. Your body and brain were designed to thrive with exercise, which has been found to improve cognitive performance, enhance memory, reverse depression, slow or stop mental decline and prevent dementia.

That sounds pretty good to me, and that's just for starters!

Unfortunately most of the exercise we are encouraged to do nowadays – spinning, treadmill and aerobics exercise – is actually detrimental to our health. It alters our body chemistry and makes us fat as it fails to build muscle, and pushes us into masculine mode, which affects our hormones. That's a whole other story!

The kind of dance I'm talking about here helps with the emotional side of life and your juicy feminine side too. This juiciness is where your body and mind are vibrantly tuned-in and turned on to life, your hormones are balanced, you look and feel at your best, well-nourished and with healthy self-esteem, and moving your body in a way that supports your energy.

Natural fluids lubricate your body so you move with fluidity and tune in to the flow of life. The movements also build new neural connections, rewiring your brain for better mood and cognitive function, making it work more smoothly and efficiently. The side effects lead to rejuvenation of the cells!

When you dance to music that inspires you, as opposed to what I call 'thumpy-pumpy' music, you also increase levels of dopamine that help you focus, and serotonin, which calms you down. It connects you with both your physicality and your feelings, which in turn increase your awareness and the sheer pleasure of being alive.

I've known many women attribute their desired loss of excess weight, their rejuvenation without the use of Botox or pills, their much-wanted pregnancy, a reversal of depression, contribution towards the remission of severe illness, and a massive change in their intimate relationships, to this form of self-expression through dance and movement, as they get more in touch with their juicy, vibrant feminine nature.

Not only that, but for business women in particular, it inspires courage, self-confidence, the joy and vitality of living, resilience, an ability to adapt more readily, to access greater wisdom from deep within, to speak up for themselves, to lead, to communicate better, to speak with calm authority in public, to express themselves better and give presentations with ease and effortlessness.

Dancing from your heart and from your body's innate intelligence will take you through to a deeper understanding and awareness of the beauty and exquisiteness of life, of your own intrinsic potency and capacity for greatness, of love, of the healing power of touch, of the joy of sensuality and the pleasure of sexuality, of connection both with yourself at a deep level and with others, which will supersede anything that words can ever do.

Words are simply not enough – the only people who can convey such feeling are poets and musicians, and so I invite you to become the poet of your own life and body, without words, without formulas, without active thinking.

A senior executive arrived at my Masculinity and Femininity weekend workshop in Amsterdam one Saturday morning, uptight, her body riddled with tension, her mind unable to switch off. She moved like an automaton, reluctant to let go, until we did certain closed-eye movements where she connected, possibly for the first time, with her inner self, and then proceeded to sob her way through much of the class. I didn't expect her to turn up for the following day's session.

However, the next morning, a woman dashed in a little late, apologising profusely. I didn't recognise her at first because gone was the grey trouser suit, scraped-back hair and drab make-up. In their place was a long flowing skirt emblazoned with colour, a pretty top and a long scarf, all which she'd bought that morning, replete with a look of utter joy on her face. She had literally let her hair down and dyed it a glorious rich curly red, and told me she'd also dropped two dress sizes overnight!

The work we'd done the previous day had been so profound that she had made some decisions about how she was living and working. She recognised that her inner self was calling out for something more fulfilling, more life-enhancing, and was already taking the steps to bring it about, realising that while she was excellent at her job, it wasn't fulfilling her in any way at a deep level, and was actually preventing her from connecting with the love inside her and from creating a relationship that would be right for her. Her protective armour literally fell away while she slept.

When your body has been held, as it were, in a straitjacket as you've tried to conform, when it is at long last given permission to move with freedom, but with specific guidelines and purpose, the locked-up, pent-up feelings which have been squashed down since childhood start to be unleashed. Tears are a familiar accompaniment as you begin to realise just how much you've hidden away beneath those old masks, and how much your spirit and authentic self yearn to be released, acknowledged and encouraged, without criticism.

I have to confess that for the first few classes when I danced with this sense of connection and freedom, I had tears streaming down my face as my body learned that it was OK to let go, to release the stress and tension and the strictures I'd felt I had to adhere to – that I wasn't going to be consumed by hell-fire and demons as the real me revealed herself. Like many others, I'd always thought everything had to be done perfectly or I was a failure. But over the years, as I've allowed the real me to be revealed, I've learned the innate perfection of each of us as individuals. Not to mention the sheer relief of *not* having to get it right, of giving my body permission to express itself in the moment, to revel in its creativity, playfulness, sensuality, sexiness and the whole passionate being who previously feared to be seen.

If we want different results, then we need to not only do things differently, but to do different things. Very frequently, even when we know what to do, we don't do it! We're always looking for that next magic pill which will solve all our problems – that next bright shiny object!

Well, I'm here to tell you that your magic pill is right inside you – it's guiding you every step of the way – you only have to listen. It's like a satellite navigation system that has been with you from your first breath on the planet. It's the wisdom of the body, which we've been taught to subdue in favour of rationale and reasoning.

In my workshops, women learn – perhaps for the first time since they were babies – to love their bodies again, to enjoy the sensuality and freedom that their bodies hold. The active ingredient here is *feeling*, and then transforming what you're feeling. Feeling and emotions are not the same.

An emotion comes from a chemical reaction triggered by an event, where the tendency is to dive deep into your thoughts and memories to make those feelings significant, where you use justification, logic and history, finding all sorts of memories to back up why those emotions should prevail. So enthusiasm, affection, lust, sadness, anger, shame, guilt, fear and joy are all emotions.

Feeling, on the other hand, is a physiological response to an outside influence and to instinct, so it will register heat, cold, shivering, discomfort, contentment, happiness, excitement, nervousness without thinking about it. It's your body's way of communicating with you, so if you're feeling anxious, look around and see what's happening in your environment. If you're stressed, are the factors causing that stress internal or external? If your body feels potent and sexy, why bother to think about it, why not just express it if it's appropriate? Feelings can be raw and powerful on multiple levels. You can even ask your body for the answers, without having to rummage through your mind! Feeling takes you to a whole different level.

The heart is even more important than we have ever given it credit for, not just for pumping around blood, but also as a seat of emotion. Recent discoveries have shown that the heart really is the seat of love and passion, as well as deep joy and pain.

In women in particular, when we talk of a broken heart, part of her heart shuts down *physically*, so it's not just romantic nonsense. Your heart plays a major role in terms of achieving behavioural change and increasing performance. You may have noticed this recently, as more and more women are willing to show their more vulnerable side when talking on stage, open to sharing what is really going on for them. This is vital for trust, as unless that authenticity shines through, quite frankly, as a leader, you're dead in the water.

Our hearts generate more electrical power than any other part of our systems, so even though there are millions of nerve cells in our brains and only a couple of hundred thousand in our hearts, electro-magnetically, our hearts generate five thousand times the electrical output of our brain which radiates out several feet beyond the confines of the body to interact with other people and their energies.

In order to pump properly, the heart has to synchronise, which is done when we breathe rhythmically. The heart has a rhythm, as does the earth. The Universe, if we were able to listen to its sounds, also has a rhythm. It is this coherence that sages and masters from times past have aimed to tune into during meditation and chanting, and that we can also tune into when we go deep inside ourselves during certain dance movements.

Rhythm is such an important part of life – everything has rhythm. In fact I tell my male clients that unless they can train their body to respond to rhythm, they will not make good lovers! Anxiety, anger and frustration all impair your performance – passion, determination and focus will enhance it.

If you have ever suffered from anxiety over your performance, you need to switch from a chaotic state of being to coherence. You can do this through long, slow rhythmic breathing to get your physiology under control, and by regulating your emotional state, encouraging the frontal lobes of your brain to work better, thereby sending better quality fuel from your heart to your brain, so you can think with greater clarity, be more insightful and perceptive and understand how to solve problems better.

Moving with rhythm is such an important thing to learn to do if it doesn't come naturally. You learn to modulate the quality of your thoughts by breathing as if through your heart, so you don't have to use masculine logic in order to bring you back to calm, clear and balanced thinking. We've all been taught to take three deep breaths to calm ourselves before giving a speech or going into an interview. Actually, what we need is to *regulate* our breathing in order to calm down. Rhythmic breath is, in fact, one of the most important elements for clarity of thought and ability to change behaviour.

Once you understand rhythm, you can surrender to the melody and harmony in life – to the music, to the dance in your day-to-day existence.

Exercise with suggested accompanying music

Breathing Dance – Athair ar Neamh – Enya

This is taken from my book *The Essence of Womanhood*, and is probably one of the most important and beautiful exercises to do to calm yourself down, to bring oxygen to your body at all levels, and to bring the rejuvenating and harmonising parasympathetic system into play. Do this before any meeting or if you're giving a presentation or before you go to work – it will be far more effective than anything else. It takes three-and-a-half minutes of joy, gets you out of the noise in your head and turns on a positive emotional state, as you open your chest and open your heart.

Ideally do this exercise standing with your feet firmly planted on the ground, about hip distance apart, with your knees and shoulders slightly relaxed. If standing with your eyes closed creates a problem for you, then sit down for this exercise.

Allow the sounds to seep into your body and with your eyes gently closed and your mouth half-open, accompanying the rise and fall of the music, slowly lifting your arms in the air like the soft curved wings of a dove as she starts out on her journey, taking your arms no higher than shoulder level, allowing your lungs to fill with air naturally, not in a forced way ... then slowly lower your arms as you effortlessly exhale.

Focus your attention on your heart and breathe in and out as if from there, allowing your arms and hands to stroke the air as they float down, soft and relaxed. Keep breathing in this way, surrendering all of your body and movements both to the rhythm and melody of the music, feeling the breath of life nurturing and nourishing your body as you breathe in pure healing energy. Breathe in joy, peace, light, love and all your heart desires. As you breathe out, release any stress or tension, worries, fears, phobias, negative thoughts and feelings, all sorrow, pain and anger, allowing yourself to be clear and refreshed for the day ahead or calm and relaxed for the night.

As the music comes to a close, rest your hands on your chest and your belly to connect with your heartbeat for a moment or two. Now slowly open your eyes and come back into the room.

'Dancing' in this way will take you under the radar of your thinking, rational brain which tries so desperately to work things out from its limited experience, to connect with your unconscious mind, inviting it to work with you at your highest level – you might even want to call this your spirit or inner wisdom or the God/Goddess part of you.

Your physiology provides streams of data in your body: for example, your stomach sends messages to your brain when it's hungry, but also is known as your second brain, as this is the focal point of what we call 'gut instinct'. As we've travelled further and further away from relating well to our bodies, so we've also forgotten how to trust this particular part of our body, but listening to it can make all the difference between success and failure.

Our emotions take the streams of data and transport them into our bodily systems – its electrical systems, chemical waves and pressure waves. This is energy in motion and can be affected by your perception and the energy behind the emotion – so if you're a drama queen, you'll make far more of any issue than is warranted. We can all make our emotions much worse if we so choose!

All the data is there but when you alter what you're thinking and change the way you're moving your body, so much of your life will also change.

Feelings are the awareness in your mind and body of these different energies. Interestingly enough, an energy may be there but you may not feel it. But your body will express it for everyone else to see. For example, anxiety has an energetic expression where you may not be able to pinpoint the source, but your body will certainly experience it: dry mouth, sweaty palms, a churning gut, a pale complexion. It's physiological. You need to tune in to what's happening at the physiological level and take control of it.

Your physiology *is* the source of your brilliance.

Your body has a sense of where all your limbs and joints are – an awareness of how you fit into the space where you are, at any one time. This is called Proprioception. By moving your limbs you literally can change the chemistry and data that floods through your body. Remember how much difference it makes when you go for a walk: it's not just the fresh air and the views, although these all contribute – it's the movement of your limbs, the oxygen and other chemicals coursing through your body as you change your physicality.

Life changes, moment by moment – nothing is ever static. When you learn to 'dance' with each stage and flow and adapt, when you soften your body and move, exchanging stiff tension with gentle fluidity, you'll shift all the chemicals and allow them to move through your body safely.

Your body loves to move. Imagine cavewoman sitting around on her bottom all day – an unlikely scenario. But imagine her walking through the meadows, climbing trees to pick fruits and nuts, digging in the soil, squatting on her haunches as she tends the fire, skinning animals and lifting heavy weights with a baby at her breast and another on her back. Now I'm not suggesting you do this(!), but your body is designed to be far more mobile than the sedentary lifestyle we tend to live. When we don't move with this fluidity, flexibility and strength, our bodies suffer and so do the states of our minds.

Just in case you are wondering, I have worked with a client who is paraplegic so unable to move any part of his body at will other than his head. When I invited him to imagine himself doing all these dances with me, his whole presence shifted as if he was actually dancing himself. The wonders of the brain and the imagination!

We are magnificently suited through aeons of development to move; your physiology is exquisitely designed for running, walking and moving in many ways, and when you fail to move, you fail to listen or hear the delicate messages, intuition and innate wisdom your body offers. Yet in the 21st century we seem to have halted progress in favour of the cerebral, but at what cost?

For example, how often do you carry on regardless when your body is calling to you to rest, is longing to go to bed and sleep, or needing some oxygen? How often do you ignore it when it's telling you to move away from someone who isn't good for you, so you override its messages for fear of being impolite or missing a business deal, when in fact if you do go ahead, it could turn out to be disastrous?

118

Your body already knows what to do for you personally. All you need to do is to become tuned in to the messages it's always been sending you about what it wants and how it can most benefit. When you tune in, you'll no longer need to be defensive – your body's natural instincts will guide you. Movement unleashes your body's energy potential and enhances your understanding of what you can do to ensure a youthful, vibrant and energetic life.

Listen to your body and follow its inherent wisdom. Marvel at the satisfaction you get when you eat food that your body actually wants, and when the movement you perform is what your body desires. You don't have to force your body to do the things that it cries out it doesn't want to do. The 'no pain, no gain' mantra which has become so prevalent in society is, in fact, a barrier which hinders the complete integration of our minds with our bodies and blocks out our emotions.

Life is calling you – listen to its invitation. When you respond, joy and vitality literally get incorporated into the cells of your body, into your blood and guts and integrated into every area of your life.

See your movements as part of the total flow of life. Ideally, spend as much time as you can out in nature, digging, gardening, being in the wild and using the natural instincts of your body. You will look and feel a million times better, and also radiate a sense of health as you do what you're naturally designed to do. Make your body come alive – feel the vitality of Life coursing through your veins and bring that back into your work! Your inner glow and radiance *will* make a difference.

Tie a scarf around your hips; find some Middle Eastern music and belly dance. It doesn't have to be perfect, just enjoy the rhythm and sensuality of the movement. Or just dance around the room barefoot with no particular steps with the pleasure you had as a little girl.

Movement unlocks our senses, makes us feel alive and allows us to rejoice in the here and now. We are physical beings, spiritual beings in a physical body, and we honour it when we allow ourselves to move in a natural fluid way. Try it for yourself and see the difference it makes!

> *"Dance, when you're broken open.*
> *Dance, if you've torn the bandage off.*
> *Dance in the middle of the fighting.*

> *Dance in your blood.*
> *Dance when you're perfectly free."*

Rumi - 13th century Persian poet, theologian, and Sufi mystic

Chapter 14
I Won't Dance - Don't Ask Me!

If at this moment you are screaming: "You must be joking. I'm not going to dance!" I'm going to ask you what your mind conjures up when it hears the word 'dance'. Is it the passion and flamboyance of flamenco, or the sultry, erotic closeness of the Argentinian tango? Or maybe the dipping and swaying of the waltz or a froth of frilly pink tutus on stage? Or perhaps the faltering steps of the famous as they subject themselves to the ordeal of *Strictly Come Dancing*?

Can you remember dancing to music as a little girl? In between climbing trees and making mud pies and playing with dolls and reading books and painting masterpieces and tinkering with anything you could get your hands on, I am sure that you danced around or had dreams of dancing.

For many women, their eyes light up as they hold themselves a little taller, a little sassier and a little more connected, away from the humdrum of everyday reality. I hear stories of how music is turned up full-blast as women dance around the kitchen or bedroom, or close the curtains and hide away while they surrender to the rhythm. Or the thrill as they talk about the sensuality of their weekly belly dancing class; or the 'dance till you drop' sweatiness of a dance-exercise class; the flirtiness of hip-hop, salsa, jazz or the nostalgia of swing. I hear confessions of: "I can't dance, but I love it anyway," or "I haven't danced for years!" "I'd love to dance, but I'm like an elephant on a dance floor," or "You wouldn't catch me doing that in public."

I'm here to tell you that *everyone* can dance! Every cell, every atom, every molecule in your body is dancing all the time in a continual ebb and flow of life, and when you join in with that dance, you'll discover an untapped wealth of joy and creativity, freedom and expression. Your body naturally loves to move – as a baby in the womb you responded to music and sound as you danced in the cushioned waters of the amniotic fluid that protected you, strengthening your limbs and expanding your awareness through movements. Movement is your natural state.

Watch any little child when music is playing – their feet begin to move, their hips begin to gyrate and their arms wave in the air, and soon they're lost in a world of vibration and rhythm, with no care as to whether they're doing it properly or not. It's as if they have no option but to dance to the beat.

Dance is one of the oldest forms of communication and expression. Tribes from all over the world still dance to the rhythm of the drum or the chant of their peoples, knowing the importance of this way of storytelling and myth that's been passed down through their culture. Both men and women dance in nomadic groups, in island villages, in mountain communities, not just for celebration, but to mark rites of passage, to grieve, to maintain the richness of their culture alive and also for the sheer joy of it – to simply express who they are.

During the dark period of slave-trading, the slaves would dance in the fields as a way of keeping supple and strong, and of sharing and secretly exploring their plans for escape, without the use of language. Many ancient forms of fighting and one-to-one combat of martial arts have now been integrated into dance form such as T'ai Chi.

The one attribute they all have in common is fluidity. Even footballers now often train using ballet and dance movements to keep themselves supple and fluid, like water.

Who knows when dance became part of human culture, but archeological evidence indicates that dance has been an important part of ceremony, rituals, celebrations and entertainment since the earliest human civilisations. 9,000-year-old paintings have been found in India at the Rock Shelters of Bhimbetka, and Egyptian tomb paintings depict dancing figures dated c. 3300 BC.

Dance, therefore, is part of our ancestral heritage. It's in our blood even if you were born and raised in a culture where dance was not predominant.

It's not only people who dance. Quantum physicists look with awe and wonder at their discoveries as they describe everything in the Universe, the planets, atoms and molecules, as participating in a cosmic dance. Nothing is static, even though it may appear to be. All is movement.

"String theory has the potential to show that all of the wondrous happenings in the Universe - from the frantic dance of sub-atomic

quarks to the stately waltz of orbiting binary stars; from the
primordial fireball of the big bang to the majestic swirl of heavenly
galaxies - are reflections of one, grand physical principle,
one master equation."

Brian Greene – Professor of Physics & Mathematics, Columbia University.
Author of *The Elegant Universe, The Fabric of the Cosmos,*
The Hidden Reality

In fact, everything you can see right now is engaged in a swirling dance of atoms – from the chair you're sitting on and the beautiful pebble you picked up from the seashore, to the metal in your computer.

"No matter how many textbooks show stationary snapshots of cells,
molecules, and atoms, it's misleading. Tiny things are actually
dynamic and perpetually changing. They are engaged in a delicate
dance that depends on how their energy fields
interact with their surroundings."

Dr. David Glowacki PhD. MA – Chemical Physicist.
Creator of Danceroom Spectroscopy

Despite the knowledge that your cells are dancing around your body, virtually everyone who has been raised in Western culture inherits a disconnection between body and spirit. As a result, we've got into the habit of treating our bodies like unconscious, inconvenient machines, rather than the vibrant vessels of incredible intelligence and emerging energies which they actually are.

And so we ignore the magnificence of our bodies and forget to tune in, unless a nagging pain or illness forces us to look more closely. This mistreating of our bodies leaves us fatigued, unfocused, stressed and depressed. You only have to look at the way women walk to see what's happening.

How much are you aware that walking with one shoulder weighted down by a heavy handbag or burdened with armfuls of 'stuff' puts your body out of kilter, as you've forgotten how to walk with your natural sway, balance and grace, with the accompanying movement of your arms?

Or that when you're cycling like a fiend in the gym, or doing a 90-minute tough aggressive workout, you're activating more of the male hormone testosterone? Or that teetering around in high heels puts strain on the balls of your feet and tension in your back and hips, let alone the lines it puts on your face as a result of sore feet – all in the name of fashion!

Added to which, sitting hunched up over your desk or steering wheel, or collapsed in a heap on the sofa trying to unwind in front of the television after a busy day, puts your body into an unnatural state for regeneration.

So much research has now been done as to the best ways of keeping your body healthy. In sessions with my private clients and at my seminars, we work with the body's sympathetic nervous system – the active energetic side – for a short time, and then allow the body to recuperate, regenerate and relax, employing the parasympathetic nervous system. The beauty of this is it works with your vitality and joyfulness followed by time to process, relax and recover, so it makes you feel good – and feeling good feels good!!!

Sadly we've been taught the: 'You have to suffer to be beautiful' mantra for far too long. I don't go along with that. When you encourage your body's flexibility through activities such as yoga, Pilates and dance, and reconnect with your body through the nourishing touch and caress of a loving massage, then your mind becomes flexible too.

The more fluid you are in your movements, the more integrated you can be in relation to other people, and able to adapt and adjust to change – something we have to be more and more adept at these days, where the only constant *is* change!

This is a state of 'beingness' rather than being stuck in the static state of "This is just the way I am!"

Life itself is fluid. The Universe is in constant motion – and unless we learn to flow with it too, we'll find ourselves, time and time again, coming up against hard blocks and unable to move forwards.

Earlier last year I spent some time in The Gambia where poverty is rife, but one of the things that struck me most was the poise and beauty of the women. Watching them walk barefoot down long, red, sandy roads, carrying babies on their backs and big plastic baskets on their heads filled with produce or bundles of fabric, the poise in their bodies, with their heads held high and hips and arms swaying in rhythm, was hypnotic to watch.

While I can't imagine us putting our shopping and computers on our heads, I observed their healthy stance and knew that we were missing out on something important in this aspect.

Fortunately, there *is* a solution – one where you literally infuse your conscious awareness back through your cells. This inner alliance allows you to access powerful sources of sustainable energy, joy and true body-felt intelligence. When you reconnect with your Body Intelligence, by default, it boosts your IQ, Emotional Intelligence and Relational Intelligence in ways that will amaze you.

Dance reawakens your senses of smell, touch and taste, allowing both intuition and greater energy to come to the fore. It helps you integrate body, mind and spirit, your determination with your intuition and your ability to move forward, your creativity with your affection, your sexual energy with your heart.

After my dance classes, I'm able to express myself in words more fluently, to think with greater clarity, to visualise with more specific detail, to follow through where previously I might have felt like giving up, to dance into my own space and welcome others in. Clients report back greater confidence and self-esteem, more pleasure in their body and sensuality, greater self-expression, a greater appreciation of life, the sheer joy of movement, a deeper connection with their spiritual side, a desire to treat themselves in a better way, to give up toxic relationships and foods and to nurture themselves in a kinder, more loving way, as well as inviting in more passionate intimate relationships!

They report having more certainty, determination and an ability to concentrate (to join their centre) better with the task in hand, but with more elegance and grace than previously. Along with an ability to express what they truly feel and to communicate with greater ease, an openness to what's going on and a deeper love for others, less self-consciousness, but with a greater consciousness of Self.

The dance I work with reunites you with your energy, vitality and life force, working with the healthy and positive part of yourself, pushing through the barriers that hold you back. It enables you to have that most essential of qualities for Feminine Leadership which we've already talked about – presence. And none of that is done through the limitations, confines and restrictions of your thoughts, no matter how hard you try, but in conjunction with your body, your cellular memory and your imagination.

Dance is a perfect metaphor for the navigational skills required of a great leader, the ability to change and adapt, to flow, to co-operate with one other person or a group, to dance with diversity, to respond to difficulties with resilience, to give healthy feedback and to express yourself with every pore of your being.

It allows you to give your cerebral cortex (the part of your brain that is responsible for thought, reasoning, memory and voluntary movement) a chance to rest, so you can dance with the unknown, kick off your shoes to connect with the ground, the earth or the sand, the carpet or the kitchen floor, and move your body with freedom and a sense of abandonment and pleasure. This is letting go, *into* life's wisdom, which we so often try to override with logic, and imprints new memories of joy into the unconscious mind.

And when you dance with others, you generate an energy of belonging, a feeling of being in a tribe, of making a difference together, of honouring and respecting each other, of seeing each other's gifts and contributions, of appreciation and the sheer joy of being alive, a levelling-out of the playing field, a true expression of life.

Ready to dance?

Chapter 15
Dancing with the Archetypes

This is where at last you actually get to kick off your shoes and dance!

If you're already good at dancing, I invite you to let go of everything you know about performance, style, steps and choreography, and return to the raw, naïve place of innocence with your movements, where you let go of anything in your head and allow your body in its infinite wisdom to take over – to experience.

Creativity is the number one 'Leadership Competency' that's vital both today and for the future, according to 1,500 top CEOs surveyed by IBM and reported by Newsweek, yet scientific measures of creativity in the USA and other countries are dwindling, just as IQ scores are going up.

As you realise by now, we cannot live by logic and brainpower alone, as it means we miss out on so much. And as we've seen, IQ alone doesn't necessarily equate to Emotional Intelligence, nor to the intelligence we need in order to not only survive, but also thrive, as a species.

"The true sign of intelligence is not knowledge but imagination."

Albert Einstein

With your time taken up just getting on with life, it's hard to fit in ways of being creative – like painting, sewing, crafts, pottery, cooking, dancing, writing, knitting, gardening, woodwork, designing new things, dreaming up new business ventures, playing music or whatever else stirs your creative juices. And all too often when you do, you're confronted by 'blank canvas syndrome' or feel stymied because there's just too much choice; and then, because you want the finished product to be perfect, that old devil, fear, in all its guises steps in and tells you you'll fail. So you pack your dreams away again until the perfect time comes along, or if you do get started, you run out of creativity time, so your project sits there, dwindling away getting covered in dust amongst the pile of other things you've not had the time to complete, as other priorities jump up to hijack your time.

So instead, how would you like to dance in the shoes of a super-powered being from time to time so you can get things done in a *different* way, to feel the potency and juiciness of your creative power, and unleash talents that you never knew even existed?

These super-powers are available to you at the flick of a switch, and you can play with them and have fun with them as well as dance between them, when appropriate situations occur.

Now I'm not suggesting you squeeze yourself into a skin-tight bodysuit and hide your identity behind yet another mask, or try to become Superwoman, because much of that is delving into masculine energy. But it *is* about employing your creativity, that spark which often lies dormant within you and doesn't often get expressed, to help you fulfil many of those unfinished dreams and express yourself in all your myriad forms of genius.

Deep inside your DNA you have access to different expressions of your inner self, which may not come to light in the general noise of daily life. But when you connect with them at a deep level, you'll find they become almost part of your team.

There already exist many different guises we show up in, as discussed in the section on masks. These are your archetypes. They are the intuitive and psychic lenses through which you view yourself and the world around you, which you can employ to help you step into the full expression of your life. Your archetypes influence almost everything you do and the way you behave.

Anything that keeps occurring over and over again is a clue as to which archetypes are operating in your life. Archetypes represent fundamental human models of experience during our evolution, and date back to the dawn of human history. Plato referred to them as 'Forms' which were later developed by Carl Gustav Jung with his work on archetypes. They play valuable roles that relate to your work, your relationships with other individuals and society, as well as your spirituality, finances, values and your highest potential. Consequentially, they evoke deep emotions, again like the masks we talked about earlier.

It's best to think of your archetypes as intimate partners or shrewd and wise companions or guides who weave their way through the tapestry of your life – through your identity, drives, feelings, beliefs, motivations, and actions. But they're not passive entities floating around in your psyche like the ghosts hovering in spooky films, either! They take on an active role as guardians and inner allies, alerting you when you're in danger of falling into destructive or 'shadow' behaviour.

There are literally hundreds of archetypes and if you research them, you'll find many which you'll realise you use on a regular basis, some which enhance your life and others which hold you back.

Effectively, they are symbols, mythologies and legends that have been handed down to us, to help us experience and understand the ecstasy, the sacredness and the celebration of life in this age where there is so much dissociation.

Each one is a representation of an aspect of ourselves which can be expressed through movement, dance, bodily awareness, emotion, personality styles, stance, voice, art, literature and mythology, to name but a few.

**Since the dawn of time, archetypal gestures or generative postures
have been revered in all cultures and civilisations
representing certain attributes of human expression.
They are often found in places of worship, representing the angelic
realm, motherhood, courage, forms of labour or love.**

Here I have chosen to work with the feminine aspects of the five major archetypes of Warrior, Magician, Lover, Mother and Sovereign as a means of enhancing your Feminine Leadership abilities. They will enable you to connect at a deeper level with your internal resources, as you start to recognise those aspects within yourself.

Trying to transform our core beliefs just using our heads doesn't work for women, because we're so centred in our emotions and have so many limiting beliefs and deep-seated conditioning, which validate that we're still not good enough. So we need more empowering methods to deal with them.

Working with the archetypes using your physicality gives you permission to access elements that you wouldn't normally be able to open up to or experience fully, yet once you taste them stirring within you, you will feel a connection deep inside to something you have always known. It gives you an indication of the power inside you, a previously experienced resource that you can call upon any time you need it, whether confronted with situations or people where you just need an extra boost, where thinking about it just isn't sufficient.

By recreating some of these archetypes through movement and dance, you can record over old memories and create new ones to take their place – memories of feeling nourished, valued and cared for, of resilience and strength, of capability and success, of tenderness and insight. It gives you greater rein to explore and use your imagination and creativity in action and you'll be enthralled by the energy and power you uncover and the shifts it will make in everyday life.

There's so much more to you that remains untapped – not only the amazing things you've already accomplished which are now in your make-up, but even greater possibilities which exist outside the concept of yourself that you currently hold, which you haven't yet encountered. So it's time to shift your sense of Self to a new level.

The exercises here work beautifully for you to practise on your own, but just as life was never designed to be lived in isolation, you need your tribe of supportive people around you, to bounce off, to reawaken and hone your instincts, which can only be accessed in the presence of others.

When you 'dance' these, you actually experience what it feels like to employ those archetypes and avail yourself of their magnificent attributes. My belief is that you are tapping into your ancestral energy which is stored in your DNA, into the symbolism and life events that your ancestors experienced, which is why you are able to recognise them in yourself. They are qualities which your forebears assimilated into their bodies and used to great effect – remember, you wouldn't be here if they hadn't!

Along with each archetype you will find exercises for your body and sometimes your voice too, so that you can feel what it is to be truly in this energy as a woman. It may feel as if you've never dared to touch these aspects of yourself before, or they may feel totally familiar to you, but once opened up you will never be content to slip back into mediocrity again, provided you keep practising them over and over again.

It's said you need to repeat something at least 21 times for it to sink into your unconscious and for you to become unconsciously competent, but I hope you will just dance them at any opportune moment, just for the sheer pleasure they bring you.

When you relax and allow the music to penetrate, your body becomes a symphony, so that the notes, rhythms and harmonies resonate with every muscle, every organ, every cell of your body, and reorganise your energy. This dramatically *impacts your physical, emotional, and mental wellbeing* so you can access your internal power and unleash your highest potential – to actualise what is there. Always with this music, please ignore all the words so you don't go into the thinking part of your mind – let them wash over you. We want to access your right brain, that well of creativity and imagination, through the rhythm, the harmony and the vibration of the music. This is about letting go of thought, and just *experiencing in the present moment* – what the late Rolando Toro, creator of the deeply transformational Biodanza system from which many of these dances were taken, called 'Vivencia'.

Rather than you dancing *to* the music, let it dance *you*. The more powerful Yang movements bring a zest, vitality and potency back into life where before there may have been mediocrity and dullness. The more gentle Yin movements of health and wellbeing where your eyes are closed, where you move from your heart, then your arms, head and rest of body, restore calm where previously there may have been anguish. Most of the music and movements here are in this realm – the realm of the parasympathetic system – a far cry from the manic, exhausting stress of continuing to work from your Yang energy.

A by-product of all these exercises is an unfathomable enhancement of your self-esteem as you give your body permission to move and express itself – as you dare to push away the confines of the ordinary.

This is where the joy, passion, beauty and dynamism of a woman comes to the fore – it will astound you as you dance into these areas of your life and harness their energies when you need them. The more you practise these, the more they become part of who you are without you having to think about it – you become them, wild and free and extraordinary as you connect with that inner part of you.

As I said before, this is just scratching the surface. When I have a roomful of people doing this extraordinary work together, wondrous things happen, and when we work in pairs or dance together in a group, the room is filled to the rafters with pleasure and fun and laughter, alongside healing tears, and deep transformation – all very feminine attributes.

There is a choice of music here – choose the one which resonates with you at the deepest level that moves you beyond your ego.

The Amazon or Warrioress Archetype

The Amazon may bring to mind a woman half-naked, having lopped off one breast and brandishing a spear. Not very appropriate for modern-day business, particularly if you're petite, wear high heels and a formal suit at work!

The Amazon tribe was a race of all-female warriors in Greek legend who engaged in fierce battle, were defenders of their family and tribe, along with nurturing their young daughters and transmitting lessons of power and self-defence. As the bearer of male warriors, it was she who taught them how to be strong, and also how to value and honour their women.

Today the Amazon or Warrioress with her strong values has emerged once again through women who fight for, liberate and protect others, especially other women, children and animals who may need vocal and financial representation.

Tapping into your Warrioress doesn't mean being a mercenary, strapping on your breastplate of armour and going out to fight. In fact, if you do it with that energy, you'll come into battle with the masculine warrior, and bloodshed will ensue, although the Warrioress will gracefully give way to those warriors who come to protect their women!

She is powerful and aware of danger. She doesn't go out and fight for the sake of it; she just has a deep inner conviction that when the warning bell sounds, she will be able to conquer and protect. The Warrioress doesn't behave like a man, but will fight to the death to defend her children, her planet, her home and her work. There may be times when you have to fight for justice, to stand your ground and not be swayed, to hold the fort and protect your business, your reputation, your colleagues, your finances, your decisions, even your body, and to be able to do so from a place of inner strength, conviction and commitment, which comes not just from the head but from every cell in your body. This is about having the capacity to express aggressivity without violence, if necessary.

The Warrioress is deeply connected with Mother Earth – she moves with freedom and instinct, listening, alert and with full awareness of what's going on around her. She notices! She has her feet planted firmly on the ground, with an understanding of the environment and what will happen if it's not tended and looked after, as she relies on the land for her existence.

She is tough, and, indeed, indomitable when necessary. The Warrioress is the one to call upon when you need resilience. She moves into her masculine energy when she needs to, then flows back into her feminine. It's not like a switch – either/or – more in the flow, like the Yin/Yang symbol.

The Warrioress is very much in touch with her body. Like an animal in the wild, she knows how to release the adrenaline in her body by moving and shaking it out of her system. She is cheeky, youthful, playful, committed, engaged, focused. She participates and calls forth participation from others. She is a leader, and great to employ when things are busy and you need to get things done, inspiring action and empowerment in others. People go to her for her vitality, her physicality and her juiciness.

So, time to kick off your shoes and turn the music up, loud!

Exercises to embody The Warrioress Archetype, with suggested music:

Dance of the Tiger – A Sweet Little Bullet – Tom Waits

The tiger is passionate, protective, dangerous, lethal even, raw, feral, wild… and also graceful, beautiful, strong, courageous, authentic – living the epitome of an instinctual life with innate primal instincts intact. And in our life too, we sometimes need that ruthlessness, to kill what's no longer needed, to go for the jugular of whatever isn't serving us any longer. And that's right – just as it should be.

Here, I'm asking you to experiment – to play with the courage of the tiger, involving the whole of your body. Feel the strength and power in your limbs as you move, as you squat down close to the ground, brandishing talons towards anything that you don't want to approach. Roar, snarl and hiss. Go on – I'm watching you!

Working Dance Out In Nature – Spirit of the Forest – Baka Beyond

If you have the opportunity to dance to this music out in nature, it will enthral you as you reconnect with the sounds of the forest, with the rhythm and beat of the earth and the call of the people. This is your body's opportunity to tap into and connect with its ancestral way of doing things, and brings us back to our natural rhythm.

Squat, imagine you are digging in your patch of earth, harvesting and gathering, moving gracefully through the trees, weaving leaves together for shelter, skinning animals, cooking at your pot on the open fire, sparks flying as you create nourishing food.

This is your ancient heritage at work reminding you of your deep inherent abilities.

Dance of Adaptability – Music Was My first Love – John Miles

The Warrioress has to be able to adapt rapidly to her environment – to be perfectly still, then to move very slowly, then with stealth and speed through the forest.

This expansive music takes you through different rhythms for you to play with, with great abandon. No special way to do it – just your way.

Fire Dance – Djobi Djoba – Gypsy Kings
or Sundance – Kitaro

As a force of nature, it's time to unleash your wild woman – deeply connected with the earth, yet able to sweep with great vivaciousness into your passionate nature like a fire.

Here you can start out with playful movements at first, then move like crackling flames, flickering, flaring, leaping. Move like a hungry serpent devouring everything in your path, then as a gentle, smoldering flame, before flashing once again into being. Roaring, eager, hungry movements as you go on the rampage and explode in a frenzy, then allowing the sparks to die down again and just be with the steadfastness of your inner flame.

Generative Stance of Valour – Eric's Theme – Vangelis

This is a gesture where you take on the pose of a valiant warrior, knowing your intrinsic self-worth and defending your honour. With eyes open and looking ahead, feet planted safely on the ground for stability, gather up energy into your hands and close your fists. Let your arms rise slowly at your sides and then cross each other across your chest protecting your heart, but a little away from your body like a knight of old, standing tall and proud and strong, letting the music seep into the pores of your being.

The Lover Archetype

Do you sometimes feel like your life force is dried up and depleted – frequently collapsing into bed in exhaustion? Or that the vibrant, adventurous passion that makes life so pleasurable has been buried under a mound of obligations and to-do lists?

Then it's time to liberate a more passionate you! A feminine being who pulses with sensual delight – who relishes everything in her path: her own self, her lover, her colleagues, her work and life itself. That's the beauty and blessing of womanhood – a life built on magnetic joy instead of heroic effort, delight instead of continual suffering, and divine power rather than ego-driven power.

The Lover may be an unexpected archetype to put into a business book on leadership, but this archetype represents great passion and devotion as well as romance. She embodies an energy of aliveness, vibrancy and vitality here, alongside tenderness, compassion, joy and laughter, and with a great capacity to love. The Lover sees the good in others, and works for the highest potential in all things and all people, and is also acutely tuned into the feelings of others.

You can be a lover of antiques, chocolate cake, music, plants, art, wealth, shoes, perfumes, children, nature or any other area of life. It's all about having a sense of uninhibited affection with a joyful and passionate appreciation of someone or something, without being obsessive.

It's time to wake up your zest and lust for life instead of this lukewarm and exhausted behavioural habit we have taken on board, along with a never-ending list of 'shoulds'. Your sexual energy is your creative life force. But we've never been taught how to align with it, revel in it and channel it as a powerful force for good. And when you disconnect with this energy, you disconnect with your excitement and enjoyment of life. You need to call it back to you and apply it to every aspect of your life, *including* business!

Because when you awaken to your full feminine essence, you become an unstoppable force – not because you try harder but because you become more radiant and magnetic. This makes all the difference in creating conscious and delicious relationships, which bring more passion and power into your life, instead of draining you. And that applies just as much to the boardroom as it does to the bedroom (although I have to confess the latter is far more fun...).

So am I talking about scarlet fingernails, raunchy underwear and killer stilettos, torrid affairs behind the water cooler, or assignations behind the photocopier? No. I'm talking about connecting with that deep sexuality, that potent sexual energy which is located in your pelvic area. This is where the creation of life starts.

The truth is that we are happier and more whole when we live in a way which aligns with our feminine energy – a vast and often misunderstood power that courses through our veins, moves through our heart, our body, our womb space and informs our sexuality.

This wonderful energy, infused with wisdom, not only charges our intimate encounters but also brings pleasure into the small moments of each day and supercharges us as leaders who are rising to the task of creating a more conscious world.

Again, I'm not talking about swinging from chandeliers, or *50 Shades of Grey* here! I'm talking about finding those pleasures in your life that stir up your juices and awaken all your senses. It may be painting a picture, playing the saxophone, dancing, being out in nature, having a glorious massage, skinny-dipping in the sea, singing in a choir, designing a garden, creating and eating a delicious meal using herbs and spices to awaken your taste buds, or making love (as opposed to having sex!) with your partner.

You see, when you bring that creative, vibrant joyfulness into your business, it will radiate out to everything you do, and *this* is what people buy: they buy people who are passionately enthusiastic about life and what they're doing!

We all need love – to be loved and to be seen. However, we've been taught to look for love outside ourselves, whereas it's inside where you will find the treasure – inside your body, inside your heart, inside your soul. As a leader, this means loving yourself enough to ensure that you take care of your own needs before tending to the needs of others – not in a selfish way, but in a way to ensure that you don't burn out.

When you cultivate more love for yourself – including your own sexual energy – you will light up a room; again that presence we've been talking about. As an aside, it's interesting to note that the most inspiring inventors and innovators on the planet – Einstein, Picasso and Chaplin, to name but a few – were renowned for having a very high sex drive and were heavily motivated by the influence of a woman. So it appears that success and a passionate, deeply sexually connected nature go hand-in-hand – and this is reflected in their work.

Believe it or not, as a woman, your pelvis determines your reality, how you're experiencing life. When your pelvis is turned on – and I don't just mean sexually, but with a movement and vibrancy that goes through all of your body – it lights you up, gives you the courage, confidence, creativity, determination and glow that makes you magnetic, connected to your core and informing your genius.

When your pelvis is turned off, which is what happens when you sit down most of the day and then just get up for a few minutes to walk to another desk, or you go to a gym and pedal furiously for 45 minutes before going home and sitting down again, your mind gets the feeling that you just don't care about your feminine energy. As a result, it just tells your pelvis to shut down. So if you're feeling grouchy and stuck, dull and listless, you need to get in touch with your Lover archetype!

As women, we walk around with so much protective tension in our pelvic area. We all carry baggage held in the body, not only from our own life and love experiences, but also inherited from our mothers and their mothers before them. As a result, we are often uptight and unable to connect and open. When you can learn to be in a place of relaxed arousal in your pelvis, in your womb space and in your vagina, it puts you in contact with your deeper emotional self, with your heart, your feminine energy and your ability to receive.

Now, in case you think I mean that you throw yourself at every available man, please don't misunderstand! When you connect deeply with your sensual self, your sexual self, there's a vibrant energy about you – one of wellbeing, creativity, youthfulness and flexibility.

When you reclaim your sexual sovereignty and independence so that you aren't reliant on others for your emotional or physical wellbeing, and you learn to ask for what you want, rather than just accept what's on offer, it sets up the possibility for greater interdependence. So whatever comes up in life, you become masterful and extremely confident and potent.

Become a sexual *being* rather than a sexual *doing*.

Ask your body what *it* wants, how it needs to move, and then go and do it! Our bodies are designed to move, and when we move with inspiring music where we become the dance rather than the dancer, we go into a place of sheer creativity without conscious thought.

The Lover is also known as the partner, friend, intimate, enthusiast, sensualist, spouse, and team-builder. People come to her to give and receive love and pleasure and to connect with life energy. Men come to her to restore their own masculine energy.

Exercises to embody The Lover Archetype, with suggested music:

Waking Up Your Pelvis – 123 Solei Khalouni – Khaled

To loosen up this amazing area of our bodies, what could be better than belly dancing or hula dancing? I suggest you tie a long scarf around your hips so you can really feel and connect with them as you move, in figures of eight, from side to side and front to back, large circular movements and playful flirty movements.

Enjoy the gyrations and sway of your body as you shimmy and improvise as you dance around your home. This isn't about performance or being good at dancing or gymnastics. In fact if you are already good at belly dancing, I invite you to let go of the form and the knowledge you have. Remember – perfection is a masculine paradigm. Just be with the music and the essence of the dance.

Allow your body to connect with the powerhouse of its sexual energy and transmute that into energy and creativity for your business and your life. Let your whole body be involved in your dance, with no judgement or self-criticism, bringing in your arms, your chest, your shoulders, your head, right to the tips of your ears and toes.

Sadly many, many women have experienced some form of trauma, particularly trauma around sexuality. Your first sexual experience will have set the tone for the future. Trauma gets caught in the body, in your cellular memory, and affects how we view the world, how we show up. If that is the case, would you like to change that, right here and right now? Because when you feel safe in your own body, you will make others feel safe in theirs – making others feel safe is another quality of Feminine Leadership.

The only way to re-pattern cellular memory is through movement and healing touch – it's difficult to do so with your brain alone or just by trying to feel love into your body parts. You must combine the awareness and sensitivity of your heart with conscious touch – this is a form of self-limbic re-imprinting and self-cellular re-imprinting that needs to be done in a gentle and compassionate way.

I invite you to go slowly, making contact with your body in a way that is opposite to trauma, so your amazing, miraculous body will re-imprint a new memory of self-care. Especially when it's connected to pleasure, your cellular memory will re-pattern.

It's time for you to completely reclaim your body, your joy, and your beautiful self.

Caress of Your Own Body – O Que Sera – Simone. Or You Are So Beautiful – Joe Cocker – Live version

This beautiful exercise is done with eyes closed, mouth half-open, ideally standing up, but you could also do it lying in bed or in the bath with the music to encourage you.

For so many women, caressing their own body is something they would never dream of doing – you may slap on the occasional bit of suntan lotion or body butter, but it's seldom done in a conscious way, unless by someone else during a massage.

This is an opportunity to learn to be loving towards your body, to caress each part very slowly… with gratitude… with no judgement or criticism… enjoying the pleasurable sensations that it produces, accepting and embracing all that you are.

It may take time to wake up those cells, for them to begin to celebrate with you, but they will, I promise – because you need to love yourself first and foremost. When you constantly criticise yourself, you will criticise everything in your own life as well as others too.

Can you imagine how it will be when you're able to walk with total confidence truly knowing just how beautiful your body is? And when you love your body, it will begin to love you back.

Therefore, caress every part of you; leave nothing out.

Learning to Say No/Yes

Some women carry around shame, guilt, repression and even worse, due to their sexual histories. We often say "Yes" when we mean "No" – or "Yes" when we mean "Not yet," or "Yes" when we're not sure. So the following is a wonderful exercise to practise over and over again. This is taken from my book *The Essence of Womanhood – re-awakening the authentic feminine.*

*Nothing is going to change in your life until you say "No" loudly enough to what you **don't** want in order to evoke an exultant "Yes" to what you **do** want, so that you then can turn your loving attention towards the "Yes." When you tell the Universe exactly what you are not prepared to put up with anymore, it will listen. Otherwise you end up sending mixed messages. Therefore make up your mind to be single-minded instead of double-minded. Wrap your entire mind around what you truly desire, and don't allow even a tiny part of it to disagree or say the opposite.*

Practise saying "No" very quietly, then increase the volume bit by bit until you're shouting the word "No!" at the top of your voice. (You might like to play some loud music so the neighbours don't come rushing in, or warn them in advance!) Use your arms and hands to express your rejection of what you don't want, to push away what is no longer acceptable to you and to your life. Now decrease the volume of your voice little by little, down to a whisper until you can say "No!" authoritatively, confidently and quietly.

Now try saying "Yes" to Life – first whispering, then progressively louder and louder until with the greatest of glee you are prepared to be all you can be, opening your arms wider and wider to embrace all the good that life has to offer.

I appreciate the fact that this may sound like that infamous orgasmic moment in the film 'When Harry Met Sally,' but that makes it even more enjoyable and fun!

Now bring the volume down until you can say "Yes!" with joy, determination, gratitude and excitement.

And now practise whispering "Yes" seductively!

Yin Dance – Cavalleria Rusticana – Mascagni;
Or Liebestraum No. 3 A Flat Major – Franz Liszt

This may well be the first time in which you've connected with your beautiful feminine essence in such a deep way, so please be gentle on yourself. Tears may flow and that's fine – they contain chemicals that heal. This is not about dancing to the rhythm or in fact using the music to be creative, but about surrendering to the sounds and your feelings.

This beautiful dance should be done with eyes gently closed and with your mouth half-open, feet shoulder distance apart and softly grounded. Allow your hands and your entire body to express the real you as you delve deeper and deeper into your feelings, and not your emotions, as this music dances you. Look for love and worth within, because this is where you will find it.

Dance of Sensuality – Europa – Gato Barbieri

Move languidly and sensually with sinuosity, like a cat or a snake connecting you to your viscera, your instincts, your sexuality, your earthiness. This ability to move with fluidity instead of in hard straight lines will help you in so many arenas of life – it will amaze you how even your mind will be more adaptable and fluid as a result. Remember to keep your mouth half-open. This will also make a tremendous difference to nurturing your body during your menstrual period, as the movement massages all your internal organs.

Flirting With Life – Feeling Love – Paula Cole;
Libertango – Astor Piazzolla; Baby, It's Cold Outside –
Ray Charles and Betty Carter

A drop of romance, a touch of raunchy eroticism and vitality all go together to awaken that lust for life to take you away from the mundane. You *are the source of your own love.*

The key here, ideally, is to do these exercises in the company of other like-minded women, or in a mixed group where the combined energy heightens their potency, and where you get a chance to practise in a safe environment – although their transformative power is still effective when done alone, don't worry!

The Mother Archetype

The Mother provides leadership inside the family holding it together with the best of her ability through thick and thin. There are things that women do naturally, such as nurturing, protecting and caring for people less fortunate, looking after children, plants and animals and putting nourishing food on the table. Even if you are not a biological mother yourself, you can hold this Mother energy within the work you do, to bring to the fore when your team isn't doing so well or if someone is unhappy, or by nurturing your partners and your business.

The Mother is considerate and fair, generous, unconditionally loving, accepting and encouraging. She is great at management, is able to multi-task and juggle many things at once, and is immensely practical. At some stage, she needs to be able to let go of what she has created, trusting that she has done the best she can, and release it out into the world rather than holding on for dear life.

The Mother archetype has a deep connection with Mother Earth. Conscious of the seasons and particularly of her own monthly cycles and hormone fluctuation, she plans her calendar accordingly and delegates at the appropriate time so she can rest up and let nature look after her. One of her concerns is what will happen seven generations into the future with anything created at this time, and she is able to tune into this with her awareness and global consciousness. She has the innate wisdom of motherhood, and has honed instincts, particularly where her flesh and blood or something to do with her business is concerned – she knows best at a *deep* level.

The Mother creates a warm hearth full of heart towards which people gravitate. She leads from a place of respect and calls forth trust and safety, support and love, inspiring others to be honourable, courageous and to be the best they can be. People come to her for safety, for succour, to be listened to, to have their hurts mended, to feel at home, to be cared for and cherished, supported and accepted.

Mother energy needs to self-nurture, otherwise she burns out. She has a deep connection with her own body, and marvels at the ability of women to grow a new life deep within.

Exercises to embody The Mother Archetype, with suggested music:

Connection with Mother Earth –
Earth Dance – To the Flame – Helen Glavin

Take off your shoes and keeping your eyes gently closed and your mouth half-open, allow the steady beat of the music to permeate your body and your soul with its rhythm and movement. Move like the ancient tribes treading softly on the earth, thanking it for its gracious beneficent blessings of food and nurture, for shelter and nourishment, for strength and power, for the ancestors who lie beneath our feet. Imagine their energy and essence willing you on, these forerunners who have gone before us to show us the way.

Feel the pulsating tribal rhythm as it connects deep within you. Feel the heartbeat of Mother Earth beneath your feet where we sow our seeds and reap our harvest. We return our waste to the soil to nourish the plants; we make love on the earth, we give birth on the earth and at the end of our lives we return to the earth.

Everything is recycled – we become the flowers and the trees, the birds and the seeds. Feel the earth's power and magnificence as you dance, allowing the pulsation of the music to take you into her entrancing energy. You may want to hunker down to the ground, kneeling or touching it as part of your dance, or even lie down to connect with the earth as the impulse grabs you.

Allow your body to become more sensitive to the rhythm and pulse of life, giving your mind permission to let go of its constant chatter and enjoy a well-earned rest!

The earth, like you, is feminine, breathing life into the planet. She creates, she engenders new life. In her fullness and voluptuousness she supports and holds us, feeds us, nourishes us, and heals us. This earthiness that we have inside us connects us deeply to our sensuality, to our sexuality and to our deepest instincts.

144

Generative Posture for The Mother – My Darling Child – Sinead O'Connor

Stand or sit with your arms crooked as if you were holding a baby and gently rocking this wondrous creature, as you gaze with love and compassion, awe and joy at your creation.

Fall in love deeply with this 'baby', whether it is a real baby or a book or a project or a business venture or your loved one, acknowledging the love that emanates from you and pours through every pore of your being.

When you connect with this energy, it will stimulate your hormones and calm you – yes, maybe tears will flow, but allow them anyway...

The Female Magician or Sorceress Archetype

This archetype is not the magician's assistant dressed in a scanty leotard, fishnet tights and high heels with a funny pout on her face. I rather like to think of her adorned in silver robes, with a beautiful hood pulled over her head and hair flowing out from underneath, with a magic wand in her hand. However you choose to picture her is fine.

It is the Magician, the Alchemist, the Sorceress, who is able to develop a vision and make things happen – she can see with her mind's eye.

The word Sorceress means 'from the Source', so she has the ability to tap into All That Is, however you may wish to call it: Universe, Creator, God, Goddess, Source, Buddha, or whatever Higher Power you connect with. She is able to manifest into reality, having one part of herself deeply connected with the earth and all its elements, while simultaneously receiving information from Source energy. She knows how to get things done with a touch of her personal magic. She learns the art of discernment and can tell truth from falsity. She is able to change her emotional state within a heartbeat as she understands the power of her emotions and how they affect her chemically, so she can use this to her advantage, knowing that changing her emotional state leads to empowerment.

She is a woman in her own right, self-contained and with amazing powers that she uses for good purposes, and an ability to transform situations with a sprinkling of magic dust. She also has deep wisdom, which she conjures up from her ancestral heritage: wisdom of the earth, wisdom of foods and herbs and crystals or medicines, together with an innate capacity for healing.

She uses her words with care, knowing that each word does indeed have a power of its own, that can make or break what she is aiming to do. She has the ability to see into the future – to see what consequences will result from her actions, and she has the foresight to stop events in their tracks if they are not sustainable and for the good of all concerned. She has the ability to slow down time or speed it up.

She can see into the hearts and minds of other people as she listens with more than just her ears: she feels the energy of the words; she feels their impact and has a *knowingness* deep inside. She fills in the gaps of unspoken words and intuitively is able to know what is going on. She understands the fundamental heart energy and how thoughts and feelings inside our hearts impact the world around us.

When you step into the energy of the Sorceress, you can transform situations into positive ones and be able to view things from different perspectives. Knowing that everything is energy, and knowing you have the ability to change – nothing is as it seems. It is only perspective and context. You can bring lightheartedness or seriousness into situations, as you have an innate ability to sense moods and atmospheres, bringing your inner wisdom to bear and an intimate knowledge of the way things work.

The Sorceress makes things happen. You charm life by loving it, rather than overpowering it.

In dealing with other people the Sorceress looks for win/win situations, but has to be careful not to be manipulative. You can raise your vitality and be playful – as the Sorceress you can also be seductive, but it's perhaps not a good idea to use these particular charms in the office!

People come to her for her seemingly age-old wisdom, her creative abilities and her connection with the numinous or mystical.

Exercises to embody The Sorceress Archetype, with suggested music:

Playful Vitality – Ai, Se Eles Me Pegam Agora – Chico Buarque

Time to be really playful here and bring out your childlike qualities of fun and adaptability. The Sorceress loves to dance around and shape-shift. Use the whole of your body: your hands, your eyes, your smile, your laughter, your breath...

Transforming Dreams into Reality – La Petite Fille de la Mer – Vangelis – or Elsha – Gheorghe Zamfir

This is a gentle walk of fluidity and creativity, moving your body with delicacy and tenderness as you act out scenarios and circumstances that you'd like to have appear in your life. This is where you wave your magic wand, sprinkling everything with a little fairy dust, and imagine – everything you touch turns, as if by magic, into reality: maybe holding a baby, going for a walk in the mountains, picking a flower, being on stage, winning an award, caressing your beloved, writing a book, floating in the sea, sailing on your yacht with the breeze in your hair, riding your horse in slow motion, playing with your children, discovering hidden treasure. This is your Invincible Vision in action.

Let your imagination soar…

Harmonic Extension – Watermark – Enya

This beautiful exercise, performed standing up or lying down, is where you extend your arms and legs just that little bit further, so you begin to realise that you are so much more than you ever knew. (Please note: this is not a gymnastics exercise, but rather, one of fluidity and grace).

Start taking up space in places where you haven't before – languidly stretching in all directions – no pressure, no effort, just gracefully listening to the wisdom of your body. See your arms and legs and your energy field reaching out further than ever before …

Dance of Fluidity – Big Blue Overture – Eric Serra

The Sorceress has the ability to slow down time – to see things, people and events in slow motion. This is being in the flow, with curved movements in your body requiring balance and harmony in each breath and movement, so that even if you were to meet an obstacle in your path, it would just be a whisper of a touch.

This exercise isn't about drifting along, but, rather, finding out where the energy is – where you feel congruent, in thought, word and deed, and where your body moves and flows as if in a sea of honey and marshmallow.

Connection with the Infinite – Shine on You Crazy Diamond Part 1 – Pink Floyd

This is another of those generative postures that have been handed down through the generations. Stand with your feet gently, yet firmly, planted on the ground, your eyes gently closed, your mouth half-open and one hand on your heart, one on your belly, connecting with the deepest part of you.

As the music swells, begin to open your eyes gently and raise them heavenwards, seeing the enormity of life around you in your awareness, bringing your arms up to embrace all that is, and slowly receiving that power and energy back down into your body.

Let this be an invitation to connect with the magnitude of the Infinite – the 'you' that goes on and on into all realms, all dimensions of being, and you will discover that you are, in fact, eternal.

Dance of Expressivity - Diamonds Are A Girl's Best Friend – Laura Fygi; New York, New York – Frank Sinatra

No instructions needed.

The Queen or the Sovereign Archetype

The Queen as an archetype has had a lot of bad press. The shadow Queen may run around barking orders, making impossible demands and cutting off heads, just as you will have seen with the Queen Bee at work or in places of authority and in many a fairy tale, or in films like *The Devil Wears Prada*.

However, here we are focusing on her beneficent aspects, which is why I prefer to call this archetype the Sovereign. Rather than being a lonely, arrogant, aggressive and defensive figure surrounded by a court filled with potential traitors, rivals, and back-stabbers waiting to usurp her position and topple her off her throne, I'd like you to look at her in a different way. Once you learn how to recognise the difference between these two possibilities, you can harness the Sovereign's constructive power while mitigating her shadow wrath.

The Sovereign is elegantly regal, serene and in command of herself and her projects but in a benevolent rather than belligerent way. She is aware of what is going on around her, is receptive, humble, gracious and omniscient, influential, concerned with social justice and has the uncanny knack of getting back to basics and common sense.

The Sovereign represents power and authority in all women and empowers others without diminishing her own. She can help you assert your power, take charge of situations, and delegate authority thus relieving some of her own pressures. Symbolically, her court can be anything from a corporation to her family and home.

The benevolent Sovereign uses her authority to protect those in her care, and sees her own empowerment enhanced by her relationships and experience. She takes responsibility for her people – she loves them and guards them, making sure that nothing will harm them. She has the ability to look at things from a different perspective, to see possibilities where others may not have see them; she is inspiring and calls forth service, loyalty and dedication from her subjects. Knowing she has been born for a higher purpose, she has a big vision for her realm, the best for her Queen-dom and is committed to serve from her higher good.

The Sovereign is generous but also knows her own boundaries. She is one of the most powerful on the chessboard of life and can move in any direction as long as it is in an unoccupied space.

She inspires others to lay down their life for her, and to provide for her, arousing respect and admiration, loyalty and dedication. People go to her for guidance, solutions, decisions and to be of service.

Exercises to embody The Sovereign Archetype, with suggested music:

Receiving Grace – Consolation in D Major – Franz Liszt

Sit down on the ground with legs crossed and hands placed on the knees, with palms facing upwards and shoulders relaxed, eyes gently closed, mouth half-open and head back in a receiving posture. This is the gift of Grace as you breathe from the bottom of your lungs gently. Nothing to do, nothing to think about, except gratitude. This inner calm is a wonderful place to work from in your life and becomes like a meditation.

Connection to Your Own Strength – Hymne à la Femme – Vangelis

This is feeling the power of your own body and life force from both inside and outside. Feel blessings bestowed on you as the Sovereign – bathe in the glory, in the energy and responsibility bestowed on you as you step into leadership here. Opening your body to receive, feeling your life grow and harmonise with what is true and honourable, moving with the music the way it inspires you, and glean from it as you move.

Creating spaces – Moonlight Serenade – Glenn Miller

The Sovereign opens spaces all around her – above, below, to the sides, in front and behind. As you allow this very feminine music to sink into your cells, move and open spaces with your arms and hands.

Sometimes it may feel almost as if you're opening curtains, other times prising apart the doors on a lift. But however you do it, allow it to be graceful and serene as you summon up the space in your life.

Then remember to step into those spaces – don't just stand on the sidelines and look at them from afar!

The Royal Road – Entrance of the Queen of Sheba

The way you walk tells its own story. This is a walk of majesty, not of ego, or showing-off or arrogance, but of acknowledgement, of pride at your achievements, of self-esteem and knowing that you are in your rightful place, centre-stage. Walk with grace, in a regal manner with head held high as if you were greeting and receiving adoration and respect from your courtiers, coming from a place of inner calm with your caring heart wide open.

Keep walking until you reach your 'throne' and sit down looking out with love and affection on your people!

Having done these exercises, I encourage you to do them over and over again until they literally become part of you, so you can call up their energy and essence whenever they are needed. They will become invaluable parts of your toolkit.

Leadership is not a role – it is a lifestyle. So when you incorporate these exercises into your life, leadership will be as natural to you as breathing.

Chapter 16
Dancing with the Dark Side

Have you noticed how in many countries the men sit and drink endless cups of coffee, often accompanied by local brandy, discussing the issues of the day, whether it is politics or football or philosophy? 'Twas ever thus since the days of Socrates. Countless others sit on mountaintops and meditate or lock themselves away in monasteries to find their truth. But this is what men often do, to find the answers, to find perfection in things, to exercise their intellect, to seek the light.

When you look at the T'ai Chi symbol, the masculine side is represented by the light section, the brightness, the sun, the fire, the powerful, the external, the logical, the reasoning, the Yang. Men are always seeking enlightenment, even if it's at the bottom of a pint of beer! It's up to us to help them now connect with their own feminine energy, their deep loving emotions, represented in the Yin-Yang symbol as a dark spot, and using their powerful Yang masculine energy, support us to create change on the planet.

The feminine, on the other hand, is represented by the dark, the night, the moon, the internal, the unseen, the emotional, the Yin, which for many years has been seen as bad and inferior in comparison. Even in personal development and spiritual arenas, we're being enticed over to the light, the masculine side, as if that were the only way to salvation. It's only very recently that I've come to realise that this continual seeking of the light is once again a place where the feminine is being rejected, where we're not seen, celebrated or honoured for who we are in our true femininity, in the depths of our emotional connection, our compassion, our passion, our joys, our distress, our caring.

My belief is that it's this separation, this rejection and disapproval of who we are in our deep juicy emotions which is contributing to the chaos we find ourselves in as women, as we constantly criticise our looks and try to change them, as we pile on the weight and stuff our emotions down, as we hold ourselves back from being magnificent leaders in the world. Never in the history of womankind has there been obesity to the extent we are now experiencing it: it's a new phenomenon.

While I know that much of this is down to poor nutrition with our foodstuffs being tampered with and taken away from their natural state, along with inadequate and incorrect exercise, I believe a lot has to do with stuffing our emotions down and comfort eating for fear of being seen, which drags us back on to a roller-coaster of low self-esteem, low confidence and hiding our brilliance.

We don't recognise how insidious and pernicious fear can be. Fear distorts how you show up in the world. We struggle so much in our own resistance – it stops you in your tracks instead of you living an inspired and inspiring life.

That little circle of light in our dark Yin is your internal bright star, that *point du départ* to light you up from within, shining brightly and with vital energy in the darkness where you emerge fully as a beacon in the world. You as a woman are uniquely designed to lead when you live the truth of who you are.

"Be as God meant you to be, and you will set the world on fire."

St. Catherine of Siena

You've got to be a source of inspiration to yourself and invest in that daily. Each of us, like the facet of a diamond, has our own calling, our own way of doing things, our own contribution, because actually *you* are the answer to someone else's prayers! What if there are people just waiting for you to show up? Yes, the natural you, with all your lumps and bumps and imperfections, because that's why we love you – the shiny, 'perfect' masculinised version isn't what we're after.

After all, there's no competition to being you, so please don't try to create something you're not. Never underestimate the difference you can make!

Your ego, the one that's currently running the show, is at best suspicious, and at worst somewhat vicious, as it hankers after perfection. Perfection, just to really push the point home, is a masculine trait that we've been taught is the path we have to follow, and again, lies on the path of resistance. My aim is to take you from aspects of self-loathing and feelings of inadequacy to acceptance and self-love.

Your essence, your authentic self, has no resistance, no fear. Your essence just wants to express herself in all her glory, to understand that your vulnerability is one of your greatest strengths, and to help you let go and trust that you've got something amazing to share. In fact it is the most selfish thing you can do – to not share who you really are!

So if you're suffering from procrastination, feminine addictions, distractions, over-planning, if you find you're isolating yourself and waiting till you get all your ducks in a row before taking action, if you're a perpetual student but not applying what you've already learned, if you self-edit, showing up in a slightly inauthentic form that feels safer than the real you, just know that these self-sabotaging and self-defeating patterns of behaviour are all symptoms of resistance!

A life-long learner learns in order to grow – a perpetual student uses it to avoid stepping out into the world and taking a stand.

What would truly showing up look like, rather than living a shadow life? Your shadow life is your unlived life, the life that seems to run on parallel tracks, but never shows up properly; so only part of you is really living.

Your shadow is always with you wherever you go, so it's time to befriend her and not simply wait for her to disappear.

We've already talked about how your unconscious mind is running the show and how to inspire it to work on autopilot in a different way, one that supports and encourages the real you. However, this shadow side, the dark side, needs a light shining on it too. You can't keep pushing it away into the corners or sweeping it under the carpet!

It's time to do a real spring clean, to fundamentally redesign the home that you live in (that's your body and your life!) and recognise and deal with the unknown, your wounding, the trauma. You need to clean up the trash, do away with the chaos, soothe the madness and heal the lurking wounds that you dare not admit to.

At this point, I want to announce in the boardroom and shout from the rooftops that your dark side, your shadow side is not evil – it's just the unlived part of you. Evil, after all, is simply 'live' spelled backwards – life un-acknowledged.

So, each time we fail to fully express the feelings of the moment, yet another bit of trauma gets tucked away into the unconscious and our cellular memory. It may not bother you on the surface of your awareness anymore, but what lies beneath is pernicious, as it seeps into the foundations of your physiology and affects everything that you touch.

Our normal response when we start to feel fear, anger or sadness is to avoid those feelings as quickly as possible, to run away in the opposite direction, or to try to drown them in food or drink or other 'drugs of choice'. Or we distract ourselves with external events. These nasty, horrible, uncomfortable, unwanted feelings threaten to throw your day and your life out of kilter, and heaven forbid if you tell anyone about them! There is a deep fear of being judged, condemned or even rejected, as we fear that vulnerability is the equivalent of weakness.

But what if it's OK to express them? What if it is actually safe to let that build-up of steam out of the pressure-cooker? I can imagine right now that you might be getting jitters in your stomach at the very idea of this, but if you look back to *A Letter to the Men* at the beginning of this book, you'll see how much it released me, how it made me feel alive, vibrant and whole again, when I stopped denying just that one part of my unexpressed self – my anger.

So too, with expressing grief. In some cultures, public grief is encouraged, with rocking and wailing and sobbing, and holding on to each other for support and succour. Here in the good ole UK and in other 'civilised' countries, we are expected to grieve for a little while privately and then carry on with our lives.

But unexpressed grief has to come out somewhere – often much later through depression, illness and even cancer.

What actually happens is that life and your unconscious mind will create circumstances for you where you may finally let your guard down and release the repressed emotions you've been carrying for so long. Something annoys, saddens, distresses or frightens you, overwhelms and threatens you and all of a sudden, it's too much. The result being that you let rip, which may not be appropriate, timely or indeed conducive to your circumstances.

So rather than distraction, suppression, denial or swallowing them back down, you need to *experience* the feelings and emotions of those old wounds. Let them flow and heal, and clean those wounds originally created way back when.

You don't have to analyse them nor lie on a sofa for 20 years pouring out your heart to a therapist. You're just getting rid of energy and the toxic chemicals that ensue, which got stuck in your cells. If you fully experience the trapped, repressed emotions and feelings, not just with your body, but with your voice as well, they no longer form part of your unconscious wounding.

When you allow yourself to heal this internal chaos by giving your emotions space to be expressed rather than avoiding them, you'll revitalise your life as you start to live from the fullness of who you are, rather than just a portion of it.

It's important here to stress that I'm not talking about wallowing in misery with your friends or discussing how bad things are. This is a deep cleansing ritual of using your body to release all that is stuck. So often if someone starts to cry, in our care and compassion we try to alleviate their pain by putting an arm around their shoulder to comfort them, but this can keep the energy trapped and unexpressed as they in turn also try not to upset you, or even worse, compete with you in degrees of dreadfulness!

Hard though it may be, it's far better for someone to get their grief and their anger out of their body. We even have a phrase for it: 'Get it out of your system.'

Your life is a mirror of what is happening in your unconscious, and if you don't address it, everything else is little more than window-dressing. Now, window dressing can be phenomenal, but we can still see *you*!

If you want change in your personal life and on the planet, if you want to live fully, if you want to bring your work out into the world, you are going to need determination, because there are a lot of wounds in the unconscious waiting for the humility and patience of the determined Warrioress to heal them. How? By crying through the pain and sadness of not being able to do it better. By raging against the machine. By expressing the trapped energy of fear from the cells of your body.

When you allow yourself to *Dance With the Dark Side*, it creates opportunities to re-train your responses away from: "I'm not going there … never in a million years!" to: "OK. I'll just dip my toe in here for a few seconds." Then, bit by bit, you enter more fully into the experience and soon discover that the world won't fall apart!

You may have already experienced that magnificent moment of standing on the edge of fear and stepping forward anyway, knowing that on the other side is a feeling of wholeness, of acknowledgement, of relief, of gratitude, of being able to move forwards.

Scenarios where your 'stuff' is brought up abound, so that you finally accept and embrace these difficult feelings, thereby setting them and yourself free.

So pause – take a deep breath – notice the emotions arising and allow them to happen! You don't have to go inside your head and analyse where they came from or try to work out their meaning.

It is a beguilingly simple dynamic. *Feel* the emotion. *Allow* the emotion. *Welcome* the emotion (especially if it feels really bad). *Express* the emotion – not *at* someone, but *with* someone – or on your own somewhere safe. Do it over and over again – but quickly without wallowing, or you will reprogramme your unconscious mind again. The idea is to get rid of it all. Cleanse your past in order to enjoy your future. Instead of blaming other people and projecting on to them and making them wrong, learn to recognise that it is something unhealed in you, always; but if you stop, tune in, feel what is arising, welcome it and give it space to be expressed, any old unresolved pain may breathe its last and be gone from your system forever!

Emotions that remain unexpressed which we don't live out fully (whatever the reason) fix themselves in us, in our body, as crystalised energy. They become areas of our lives with which we dissociate – in other words, they live a life almost separate from us but yet still having enormous influence deep in our unconscious mind where they lurk, ready to spring up at any time unbidden because they've neither been listened to nor acknowledged.

Remember, your unconscious mind runs the show! We may not be able to work out what our wounds are, but other people can see them – the pain shows in the depths of our eyes, in the way we breathe, in the way we carry our bodies.

These dissociated emotions, those buttons that get pressed, get triggered so often at work and in relationships, where we dare not speak our truth for fear of rejection. The problem is, they get stuffed down into our cells so deeply that even *we* may not be able to access them until they arise in a particular situation, such as during a massage, while in a place of utter beauty or while making love.

Consequently, these pieces of ourselves are abandoned, lost in the vastness of our unconscious and limit the expression of our potential, the expansion of our creativity, and deny access to a state of abundance. They limit our possibilities to do what we are here to do in the world. They need out!

> *"We rarely hear the inward music but we're*
> *all dancing to it nevertheless."*

Rumi - 13th century Persian poet, theologian, and Sufi mystic

If you want to live your life fully, you need to descend to the darkness, to the pit of despair, the dark night of the soul, to clear out these deep-seated hurts and wounds.

Like a tree that in order to bear beautiful fruit has to sink its roots deep into the earth, so too, we need to go deep down, right to the core of it all. You need courage to do this work – the rage of the heart – to release those things that you had hoped to achieve, and realise they are just not all going to be done in your lifetime, and deem them complete. And to just be with whatever turns up – together with a large box of hankies!

The majority of psychotherapy is Yang-based, as is our education system. That dynamic powerful masculine Yang energy is vital for launching a product into the world, in whatever form that takes, and also to have the determination to see it through. But it's the Yin, the healing, soothing gentleness and acceptance of your feminine side, the side that you may not often have revealed, that will nurture and contain you.

Just to give you an example: put on some loud music and shake your body all over, shake those emotions and feelings out! Just shifting your physical body will move them around, away from being stuck. Play music which varies in tempo and rhythm – any movement will do, as long as it involves all your body, not just your arms and legs but your hips, your head and neck, your back, your shoulders, your fingertips, right down to the tips of your ears.

The more you release, the more energy and vitality you'll find returning to your body. Allow gut-wrenching sobs and a torrent of tears; you'll find such power and joy and excitement for the future, as you become more of who you really are.

Play loud Dixieland music – go wild! It is said, "Hard times require furious dancing!" Well, we're living in hard times, and this world needs some furious dancers!

When we work with these clearing movements and dances in my workshops, the power and energy that gets released is phenomenal, and people feed back to me how energised and free they are after many years of holding it all in.

So, having finished this active dance, now go and soothe yourself lovingly with beautiful music, where you caress your body all over the way you would like to be touched, to continue to heal those wounded parts.

Leadership requires that you work on your 'issues' and heal them. What better way than to dance them out!

Chapter 17

Becoming the Mistress of Your Mind

There are myriad books already published on mindfulness and how to use more of your mind, so I don't want to dwell too much on it here, except to touch on a few salient points: remember 95-99% of all thoughts that pass through your head don't actually belong to you – they are passed on to you by society, parents, schooling, religions, by the people you hang around with and by the media.

It's reckoned that each of us have between 55-60,000 thoughts a day and that most of those are the same ones we thought the day before, and the day before that, and so on. In other words, most of our thoughts don't originate with us. Similarly, most of our memories are distorted, deleted and generalised because of our conditioning and belief systems and the way our mind filters memories. Therefore, most of what goes on in our heads either doesn't belong to us, or isn't really true anyway!

So we're going to take advantage of that fact that nothing is quite as it seems, and embroider some of your memories so they become like a beautiful tapestry. Instead of putting them away in the bottom drawer like old family treasures, we're going to call these 'Top Drawer Memories', so they'll be the ones you first turn to, to keep you elevated and full of the joys, to keep you on track for success and stop you having to work so hard! It's time for you to become the Mistress of Your own Mind rather than letting your mind take control over you.

The phrase 'top-drawer' was initially used to denote a person's level of social standing, based on their family background. Families were either 'top-drawer' or belonged to lower social strata. The top drawer is also the highest drawer of a bedroom chest of drawers, where Victorian gentry kept their most valuable items: jewellery and their finest satins, silks and special mementos.

Remember the neural pathways we talked about earlier? The more often you recall your own Top Drawer Memories, and even better, the more often you act them out so they become embodied – in other words your body has the muscle memory and cellular memory of what they actually *feel* like – the more your unconscious mind will accept them as true, and new neural pathways will be created and old ones strengthened. After all, you believe all that rubbish you tell yourself about not being good enough, not having enough qualifications, not being young enough or old enough or wise enough or clever enough or slim enough or beautiful enough; so why not reverse that and help you take on board how magnificent you *really* are?

So for starters, let's create five examples – you may want to choose different ones of your own:

1. Looking good and feeling successful.

2. Feeling wealthy.

3. Being really happy.

4. Loving and feeling loved.

5. Feeling healthy.

This is a powerful exercise to go back and rewrite your personal her-story. Your unconscious mind doesn't know the difference between what is fact and what is fiction – it will just run on whatever you present it with, whatever is the most prominent programme in your mind, and the one you run the most.

So how about stopping running the bad ones and replacing them with only good ones? Our minds are unimaginably powerful and have tremendous creative power. As I have said before, there is a growing body of evidence that what we call *feeling* may be the most powerful creative force known to us, and that our lives respond to the template of what we *feel* and not just what we think, which is also why the chapter on *Dancing the Archetypes* is so incredibly powerful and effective.

And so I want you to bring back all the memories you can associate with looking good and feeling successful.

Perhaps it's a time when you were going somewhere special, or you were delivering a business presentation, when you looked in the mirror and were able to admire yourself with no negative feelings of judgement at all. You just knew you looked great; you were feeling delicious, feeling sexy.

Now I want you to bring back the memories of *seeing* yourself positively (V=Visual). Bring back everything you saw, the colours, the shapes, the textures, the brightness, and really be *in your body* experiencing this. Now think of another time when you looked fabulous; maybe you'd just had your hair done and you loved your new look. And that time when you caught a glimpse of yourself in a shop window and you thought *You're doing OK, kiddo!* Keep bringing up the memories, all the way through your life – those little split seconds when you felt good. Maybe you had new shoes and were excited, or new underwear or a new frock. Maybe you were getting ready for a party. Maybe it was your wedding or a special birthday.

Now hear what you were saying to yourself inside your head (A=Auditory), all the good things you liked: your make-up, your smile, the glow on your cheeks, the twinkle in your eye, perhaps the voices and words of other people admiring you. Maybe there were sounds in the room or in the environment, people's laughter as they enjoyed themselves, music, bird song, the sound of the waves in the distance. Bring them back like the sound track on a movie.

Now how you felt both emotionally (Ki=Kinesthetic Internally), feeling delicious and sexy and strong and powerful and in your own skin, confident and excited; and (Ke=Kinesthetic Externally), the temperature on your skin, whether you felt warm and cosy by a log fire, or outside in the sunshine or with a breeze, the feel of fabric on your skin, the tingle of excitement running through your body.

Now the smells associated with that time (O=Olfactory). Maybe you were wearing a perfume, or there was the scent of flowers in the air; or the smell of delicious food wafting its way across the room, or a bonfire in the garden or the acrid smell of fireworks, or the smell of newly mown grass.

And maybe a taste associated with this time (G=Gustatory). Champagne and smoked salmon, that tang of lemon juice and the pungent piquancy of black pepper, the creamy texture of yummy pudding or the melt-in-your-mouth silkiness of dark chocolate, or a delicious freshly squeezed juice or whatever tantalised your taste buds.

Now keep bringing back all these scenes, lots and lots of them. Bundle them all together, and keep playing them through one after the other like a film on the screen of your mind, where you are the main actress seeing things through your own eyes, using V-A-Ki-Ke-G-O, over and over again,

163

just holding each part of that memory for 15-17 seconds each. Make each one brighter, sharper, more colourful, and even more sensual. Magnify it so it becomes even better; make it more fulfilling, more wonderful, more joyful, more fun.

Now, rewrite the script exactly as you would love it to have been if you were the heroine of your own story. Exaggerate it and step into that scene, embracing it fully with your presence *as if you were there right now*.

Put your body in those positions of admiring yourself, or being on stage, or holding that gorgeous smiling baby or winning that award, or seeing all that money in your bank account or being invited on board that yacht or that wonderful holiday in Italy or Hawaii, or being caressed all over by your delicious lover.

Describe it out loud and be there – be present. Walk it, act it, dance it. Move your body to feel those same feelings flooding through you.

Now with all those juicy hormones flooding through your body, write it out on paper with as much detail as you can possibly muster, all those positive energising magical 'memories' with never a negative thought to get in the way, and as if it were happening right now, not in the past. No justifying and contradictions or "Yeah buts." Maybe you were on stage and had just finished a presentation and the audience responded really well to your words. In fact as you recall, they were all standing up and clapping with beaming smiles all over their faces. Embroider it just like a tapestry until you are indeed glowing.

Now do the same with a time you were feeling wonderfully loved and loving, a time where you were feeling wealthy and abundant with money flowing in – perhaps you can see a big fat cheque or lots of money in your account. Make it bigger, change the numbers – keep installing this scene in your mind so it becomes like a fabulous film you can play over and over again. Rewrite those old memories the way you would like them to have been, and keep reading them over and over again so that a new memory can emerge. You can take out the people involved and the places and replace with whatever you desire. You become the scriptwriter in the film of your life.

Put yourself in the place of a film heroine's story, to suit your life, in an Oscar-winning performance! Putting *these* images in your autopilot, to replace those old negative patterns of thought will make such a difference to how your life starts to play out.

"But it's not true!" I can hear you say. Let me remind you that your mind makes up things all the time anyway, as it distorts, deletes and generalises, so why not enhance some of these details too? If I told you that this were a matter of life or death, would you do it? Well, in a way it is. It's a matter of *your life*. You see the tendency, particularly for us as women, is to find the bad stuff to put our attention on as it makes us feel we fit in. We forget to celebrate our achievements, no matter how big or small, and rush off to the next thing on our to-do list, while still feeling inadequate! Here is the chance to acknowledge the greatness of who you are. Forget the negative stuff – it's only a misguided perception.

If your neo-cortex, which is the thinking part of your brain, is constantly creating negative messages about your life and the world in general, your brain stem will continue to generate a negative response for your body. Responding to the alarm generated by your brain when you judge yourself or compare yourself or just beat yourself up, your sympathetic nervous system puts your body into the fight or flight state, which increases your heart rate, brings tension to your muscles, and generates a host of other bodily effects.

The parasympathetic nervous system is waiting in the background to return your body to the 'rest and digest' state, but if you can't learn to quiet the messages of alarm from the neo-cortex through changing your thoughts and your physiology, you will be left in an almost constant state of stress. Eventually, the stress response creates great wear and tear on the body, and this is how many stress-related problems come about, because the brain stem is never permitted to create balance in the body.

As you learn to clear your mind of extraneous negative thoughts, you'll also learn to shake off burdensome emotional memories by replacing them with your new Top Drawer Memories.

Your mind will become clearer, and you'll be able to access your full creative potential. As you empty it of old debilitating thought patterns, you'll discover new ways of approaching problems and limitations. And as you send positive messages to yourself, you'll also gain a new sense of self-worth.

Re-enact the same scenario with each of the other categories – when you felt wonderfully fit and healthy, the exhilaration of feeling successful when you won an award (particularly if you were only a child at the time), or when you completed a project that you were really proud of. Put all these memories together and keep pouring them into your mind so that you can call on any of these exuberant memories when you need back-up support!

Stick a copy of your writing on the inside door of your wardrobe, put it in your underwear drawer or in your purse, just to keep reminding yourself how you can feel. Record it on to a voice recorder so you can listen to it over and over again while you are travelling to work or in the bath.

This is a marvellous exercise to do when you first wake up in the morning, in that state between being asleep and fully awake – when your mind is open to imprint its first thoughts and create the day as you mean to go on. Flood your mind with at least three of these Top Drawer Memories as you wake up and put your body into those same positions – literally dance your wonderful memories – you don't need music.

Whenever any old disempowering patterns of thought pop up when you least expect them, immediately reach for one of your Top Drawer Memories. It might be just as simple as running your fingers through your hair or stroking your belly or touching your ear so that those memories come flooding back into your body. Or moving your shoulders in a different position or just stretching gently or a quick swivel of your hips to help remind you.

Now I invite you to go back to *Dancing the Archetypes* and dance them again with these new energies and memories.

Chapter 18
Dancing Backwards in High Heels

Time to put your Invincible Vision into action.

Have you, like me, been taught Goal Setting 101 and also the SMART (Specific, Measurable, Achievable, Relevant and Time-Bound) methodology that goes with it? Well, that blinkered, total focus works perfectly for the male brain but is overly structured for a female brain, purely because we are blessed with diffuse awareness.

This means that we have an awareness that goes way, way, beyond our visual field, so while men have a single focus when faced with a task in hand, we literally pour our attention on *everything*. In other words, unless we employ our masculine Yang energy, we don't focus.

Rather than think of this as a disadvantage, this diffuse awareness has enabled our survival as a species as women have been able to sense, perceive and see things in our environment that would have otherwise been harmful to us. Just notice all the details you pick up in contrast to a man's view when describing the same event! As women, all too frequently, if we fail to achieve our goals, we feel we are a failure, whereas actually it's the system which has failed us, quite simply because it doesn't work with the way we use our female brains.

Women are aware of not only what our eyes can see in front of us, but also seem to have eyes in the back of our heads and ears, and also all over our bodies as we hear and sense the world around us in a 360-degree fashion, rather like the hearing of a dog and the multi-lensed eyes of a bee or a fly. It's not just a visual and auditory ability; it's sensory, too.

Diffuse awareness means that we sense and pick up things and energies in our environment that are way outside those that a man can sense. Some call our diffuse awareness 'intuition', but it's even more than that. While men think we are distracted (and that is a distinct possibility as things in our environment literally and metaphorically seem to talk to us, demanding our attention!) diffuse awareness enables us to see potential problems and also potential solutions, as we are less one-track-minded.

While the male eye is more sensitive to small details and moving objects (gazelle and wild boar anyone?) the female eye is more perceptive to colour changes (so we could tell whether berries were ripe and good for us), more sensitive to sound (mosquitoes and mice approaching!) and more sensitive to smell (is that your man entering the cave or a man from a marauding tribe?).

Can you see how this works so incredibly well when *partnered* with a masculine perspective? Together we create a whole (holistic) way of looking at the world and solving problems.

Remember, your ancestral attributes were a matter of life and death, but we're now losing the instincts to distinguish these important attributes for survival in our modern world, much to our detriment. We're bombarded at every turn by so much information that our brains can't take it all in – just think of all the colour, sound, smell, vibration, tastes and textures that greet you at any given moment as you walk through your town or city, let alone those which have been manufactured so that our natural instincts are dulled, such as deodorants, perfumes, CGI in films, along with artificial colours and flavours in our foods.

Rather than be on the cutting edge, I believe we need to be on the creative edge. Your *mind* is your creative edge, so I've come up with what I call 'The Sorceress Solution'. No, it's nothing to do with magic wands and witches although it may seem like it; it means becoming, and staying connected to your Source, the highest part of you.

Using this approach has led me to do things I had previously only imagined in my wildest dreams – having my own radio show, filming a television series at Pinewood Studios, travelling around the world running leadership and training workshops, speaking on stage in front of hundreds of people; in short, thriving as a 21st century woman.

I've been fortunate enough to have met and worked with some of the most extraordinary people to grace this planet, I have three wonderful children and two adorable grandsons, supportive, loving relationships, and my health gets stronger every day. I also have an incredible group of friends whom I love dearly and who keep me on my toes if they see me slipping back into old non-supportive habits!

I love my life and even though things go horribly wrong from time to time, I know and trust that somewhere there are solutions that I just haven't found yet. And I know that more and more amazing things are opening up to me all the time.

I transform when I work – I come into my own. Light shines through every pore of my being and I just love what I do. For years I worked so hard, pushing forward, trying to achieve my goals, burning out *en route*, until I learned this other way – of working backwards.

And if it's good enough for Ginger Rogers, it's good enough for me!

"Sure he (Fred Astaire) was great, but don't forget that Ginger Rogers did everything he did, backwards … and in high heels."

Robert Thaves (1924 – 2006) Creator of the comic strip Frank and Ernest

The Sorceress Solution invites you to start with your outcome – what I like to call 'aspirations for your Inspiring Vision' (as opposed to the more masculine version of goals, targets, etc.) and work backwards from your success *as if it has already come about*.

As I was writing this section, I was invited to a lecture by one of the riggers behind the Oscar-winning film *Gravity* to see how they used computer technology to put the film together. It was 95% computer-generated and unusually, he said, they made the film backwards. They filmed the body of the film first, then put the characters in when the main film was completed, then added the finer details and the lighting. Exactly what I am recommending you do here with your Invincible Vision.

Typical masculine energy is outward, driven, competitive, focused, targeted, exclusive, solution-oriented, tunnel-visioned, and forward thrusting. In contrast, your potent and powerful feminine energy draws towards itself, is inward, receptive, magnetic, collaborative and inclusive, where you can see everything and everyone around you.

Women understand the impact and implications of aggressive competitiveness as we've all experienced it, mainly to our detriment. The feminine has this incredible capacity to see the bigger picture in fine detail, so we're now starting to embrace true sisterhood and help each other and collaborate as women. We metaphorically 'birth' our businesses – it's like our soul work – so when we look at them from that perspective, nourishing and growing our work, rather than thrusting it out into the limelight, it becomes special and life changing.

The Sorceress makes decisions with her heart. Remember that your mind is just like a computer, a tool that you can turn on and off, while your heart and your womb-space are where your understanding and intuition reside. You can use your head to carry out everything your heart and your feminine knowingness desires and intuits, so you are in fact blending the two energies of Yin and Yang. When you come from these spaces, which bypass the logic of the mind, we actually make it more socially acceptable for men to be in their hearts too.

The Sorceress Solution

Step 1
Know Your Outcome

Most people spend more time planning their new kitchen than they do their lives. However, the very fact that you're reading this means that is about to change!

Many of my clients, when I ask them what they want from their lives, come out with a whole list of what they *don't* want, ranging from work to partners to the way they view their body – you name it, they say it. However, the more you focus on what you don't want, the more you get – exactly what you don't want.

So Step 1 is to set your outcome and be very clear about exactly what it is you do want. Don't be wishy-washy here. Clarity is key – but this comes from the heart, not from your head. What really matters to you, not anyone else, but you? What are your aspirations? What do you dream of achieving? So this is the detailed description of your life the way you would truly love it to be: your Inspired Invincible Vision in detail.

It's important here that you write your answers down on paper and keep on writing until you've poured your whole heart out.

Question 1

If you achieved this outcome, other than the pleasure and gratification of having achieved it, what else would it give you, cause to happen in your life or create for you?

Question 2

If you achieved this outcome, what *wouldn't* it give you? What would not happen as a result, what would not be created?

What we're looking for here is absolute congruency and alignment. So if there are *any* negative consequences that might occur as a result of achieving your dream or outcome, you need to dissolve these away completely or select another outcome. Otherwise you run the risk of sabotaging yourself – something we're actually quite good at!

You have to be so congruent with what it is you desire that there's nothing left to wrong-foot you. If, for example, you truly desire to have a healthy body, you wouldn't fill the kitchen with boxes of biscuits, crisps and take-away pizzas and sit on the sofa all day stuffing your face!

You need to have a really powerful reason as to *why* you want your particular outcome or aspiration. Quite simply, if your reason 'why' is sufficiently strong, the 'how' will be so much easier. Your 'why' is like the emotional rocket-fuel to achieve your desire – it could be so that you can see your children grow up so you enjoy the pleasures of being a grandmother, or of being able to travel and see the world. Or becoming CEO of a sustainable business that supports the environment. Or heading a charity that makes a difference. Or starting your own business that expresses your passions and talents, and taking that out into the world. This may change the outcome of the exercise you did in the chapter *What on Earth Are You Doing?*

For example, if you need to protect your loved ones, your emotional drive will be so strong that the 'how' won't matter – you'll just find a way of doing it.

If you look back through history, everyone who has ever achieved something spectacular has done so because they had a strong purpose, a strong 'why'. At the cognitive level, having a strong sense of purpose is one of the propelling forces that will drive you towards attaining it. You don't need motivation for this, you need *inspiration* – the highest quality fuel for life. I know when I dance with abandon, letting my soul soar with the music, I become so inspired to get on with things, to be creative, to write, to share with people, as if all my creative juices were waking up.   •

Who else could benefit from your success? It could be a loved one, your whole family, your business, your community, your country or the entire world. You could become a beacon of success for others, so make your outcome something that will benefit others as well. Be generous – don't let your 'why' be just about yourself!

Once inspiration takes hold of you, you can add as much detail to your outcome as you like. So now get it out of your head and on to paper and in technicolor detail, using the V-A-Ki-Ke-G-O system I shared with you earlier. If you can see, sense and feel what you desire in your mind, it will manifest into your physical reality. This is the law of quantum physics, and it is *guaranteed* to happen if is within the realms of possibility. I'm sure I don't have to spell out that if you want to be an opera singer and you're tone-deaf, chances are you won't fulfil that particular one. And if you're 103, winning the marathon may be out of the question too... but of course, I may be wrong!

Make a strong decision that this is it – no airy-fairy nonsense here.

Where you put your attention is where you put your energy. When you put your energy on a future event, your body will be drawn to that experience. So be a woman of substance – make sure this is what you really, really want. It's like ordering from a menu, but you have to do it with certainty, and make sure you notice when it turns up!

Step 2
Stretch Your Outcome

Now, in the same way you stretch your body, stretch what you desire, because somehow we never quite imagine big enough or with enough vibrancy. As the saying goes, "Reach for the moon – even if you miss, you'll land among the stars." So make your aspirations bigger and grander and even more dynamic. Don't bore your brain cells with mediocrity – feed them so they too can dance with adventurous, vibrant, inspirational magic and imprint them on the fertile soil of your mind. Then you have the potential to fly!

A note here: Sometimes we hold back thinking we don't deserve, or for fear that we won't attain what we want if we stretch our imaginations too far. Sometimes too, we hold back in case our desire means that someone else may be ousted out of a job, or that Great Aunt Harriet may die if we imagine having lots of money.

Therefore, at the end of your list add: 'or something better' and 'for the greatest good of all concerned'.

> *"(Wo)Man's mind, once stretched by a new idea,*
> *never regains its original dimensions."*

Oliver Wendell Holmes (1809 – 1894) American physician, poet, professor, lecturer, and author based in Boston

Step 3
Imprint your unconscious mind with your desires

There are many ways to do this – using vision boards, writing out your desires with passion, recording them with your own voice and listening to them every night before you sleep and first thing in the morning when you wake up, reciting them so they get recorded into your muscle memory, or dancing them out as I talk about in this book.

However you do it, you must do it with emotional intensity, as if it were happening right now so you feel powerful and magnificent!

Step 4
Dance backwards

Have a conversation with a friend. Imagine it is a year from now and you have already achieved many of the outcomes in your vision. Tell her (as if it has already happened) the details of what you did to get there. Animate your voice, your gestures and your expression, in order to keep imprinting this into your unconscious mind. Remember, the mind doesn't know the difference between what is real and what is imaginary anyway, so it will take it on board like a programme.

Step 5
Let go of attachment to your outcome

When I first ventured into the personal development arena when everything was taught by strong-minded men, I took on board all the aspects of their behaviours and became very good at being a pseudo-man. I also took on their ideas for all the things you were supposed to want, so my vision boards had expensive yachts and planes and villas that became my goals to own. I could feel part of my mind was rebelling against some of them, but because everyone else was urging each other on with these enormous visions, I felt I had to join in with the crowd too (not a good idea by the way!).

When I eventually let go of the Yang energy of these, I started to listen to my heart and realised it was the *experiences* I was after, not the ownership of these expensive toys. Once I'd changed my vision accordingly, I was being whisked away on beautiful yachts (where I didn't have to scrub the barnacles off the bottoms!); I flew over the volcanoes in Hawaii on small planes for which I didn't have to pay hangar fees; I helicoptered over the turquoise blue waters of the Whitsunday Islands in the Great Barrier Reef in Australia and was given the joystick to steer; I went whale-watching and swam with dolphins; trekked on elephants in the jungle; stayed with tribal families in the mountains of Thailand; and went orchid-hunting in the rainforest in Brazil with the native aboriginal Indians, where no man had trodden before.

Later, I became part owner of a magnificent manor house in the Cotswolds in the UK where I now run courses and wonderful retreats. I bought my ideal home, which went above and beyond the designs in my own mind, and even though I've now moved on, I had ten years of waking up in that house with such joy and gratitude.

So listen to your heart, and also don't keep going back to check that your aspirations are growing. Like a plant, once the seed has been sown, there's no need to dig it up from its pot to check the roots. Let go of any anxiety about it and get on with your life, being open to the circumstances that come your way that can lead you closer to your desires.

Step 6
Be the best you can be!

This applies to everything you do, whether you're polishing a table or leading a team. Being your best doesn't need to be hard work – it just becomes a part of who you are, without being fanatical about the results. When you're being the best you, you inspire others to be their best selves, too.

So pour your heart and soul into what you do – because living in a lukewarm way is a very dull way to live. Rather than just living a peaceful life, why not live a life of intensity? When you do what you love and love what you do, AND get paid for it, then you are very blessed indeed.

Dare to live!

Chapter 19
Radical Self-Care

If you've danced the exercises in this book so far, you'll already have noticed that your attitude and behaviour towards yourself and your body have changed as you've begun to nurture yourself in a different way.

Being close to burnout is a wake-up call. In fact, it's a gift, as it gives you the opportunity to reconnect with your inner guidance system and work out what's really important to you in life, including asking yourself the questions, "What's happening that I need to be aware of? What can I do to change this? What do I want to be different? What are the results I want?"

It's estimated that about 85% of people in Western society are suffering from stress-related illness, leading to emotional exhaustion and physical depletion. Yet deep inside us lies an innate ability to heal. You have within your body the most perfect pharmacy to bring your body and mind back to equilibrium, if you just knew how to access it.

A certain amount of stress is useful for us, otherwise we'd all be flopping around like stranded jellyfish on a beach! However, each of us has different indications as to what it feels like when we're headed for burnout, and there is also plenty of information on the Internet with all the warning signs. If any of these apply to you, then please, please, listen to your body. It has aeons of wisdom in it. If you're willing to pay attention when you see yourself sliding down this slippery slope, it's better to do something about it *now*. In order to be women of power and of love, we have got to learn to pay attention. It's all about awareness, about choices.

For myself, I know my red flag warning signals are:

- A very unpleasant buzzing sensation in my solar plexus, as if plugged into the electricity supply;

- My head feels as if it is about to burst, not with pain but with too much 'stuff';

- I hold my body in tension as if I'm afraid that if I let go, my whole world will collapse;

- I forget to eat at sensible times, and then start stuffing myself with carbohydrates, telling myself I need the fuel;

- Getting to sleep is difficult and I wake in the middle of the night unable to get back to sleep;

- My mind races round the hamster wheel each night and will not calm down;

- Alcohol becomes far too appealing;

- Exercise and fresh air become things I will deal with 'later' when my endless to-do list is completed;

- I overwork, pushing through the fog of fatigue to not only my second wind but also my third wind as 'I have to finish' what I'm working on, at all costs. (Remember here that the 'cost' is very high!);

- I put another protective layer of fat on my body;

- My digestive system gets compromised;

- I forget to tune in to my energy resources – such as good food, water, having a nap, fresh air, dancing;

- I tend to hibernate, where I cut off from my supportive friends;

- I glue myself to my computer and forget to take a break;

- I ignore the nutritional supplements that sit in my kitchen cupboard;

- I get very defensive with people around me;

- I don't bother with make-up or dressing nicely;

- My libido and my sense of humour go out of the window;

And this is probably only the beginning. Other warning signs are there as well.

I don't want to insult your intelligence by listing things that you already know about, BUT – and it is a very big but – so often, we take great pains to accumulate vast amounts of practical knowledge, but never really apply it. We take pride in the fact that we read the book or attended the seminar, but we fail to carry out everything we've learned.

The Buddhists have a proverb:

"To know and not to do is not yet to know."

It's time to birth a new way of being, and of developing resilience with grace, humour and elegance in these fast-paced times of change. You can't be of service to yourself or anyone else if you burn out. If you want to love, care for and be there for others, you have to love, care for, and be there for yourself *first*.

This body of yours is the sacred temple in which you have the privilege to spend this all too brief lifetime, and it is often not until things begin to break down that we give it the attention and care it so deserves. And when you skip over the foundations of self-care, chances are you will end up exhausted.

This masquerades at first as stress or even a modicum of depression but can swiftly move on to burnout. If you let yourself burn out in service to this conscious evolution that is happening around the world right now, you swiftly become unconscious. Most of us here right now are overly busy, stressed, overwhelmed with information and with a to-do list that seems never-ending. We keep our nose to the grindstone working harder and harder, promising ourselves a break just when we finish this next bit, but in truth the wheel keeps on turning. So you have to take stock.

Your to-do list will never be done. Sorry, but that's the truth! You won't get it all done in one lifetime, so be gentle on yourself! I need to reiterate here too that those of us who want to change the world so badly are often the most prone to burnout, as we have this all-consuming passionate desire deep inside that threatens to overwhelm us sometimes, while other people seem to be content to just sleepwalk their way through life.

Even as I have been writing this book, there have been times when I've felt somewhat jaded and, quite frankly, stressed and overwhelmed, as circumstances around me have pushed me into looking after others first and relegating myself to the bottom of the list. And in all that, I forgot to dance! So it became a question of 'Physician, heal thyself!'

A friend asked me when she saw me in the hospital waiting room, "What's the one thing you teach that you're not doing?" (Duh!) In my passionate desire to get this book out into the world, I wasn't taking my own medicine. So now, if even the beginnings of those feelings start to stir within my body, off come the shoes, on goes the music, and my body thrills to the movement as I change my physiology, and the happy creative hormones come flooding in to rescue me again.

Confucius said the same thing too:

> *"I hear and I forget.*
> *I see and I remember.*
> *I do and I understand."*

Psychologist Hermann Ebbinghaus created what is now known as 'The Ebbinghaus Forgetting Curve' which suggests that unless we actually practise what we have learned, we forget it very rapidly. Which is why information doesn't stay in your brain very long after reading it; or why most seminars where you are just sitting listening to information only have a short-term effect. Hence another reason why actually *doing* the dances and exercises in this book will change your physiology and chemistry, and will remain with you, embedded in your cells.

I invite you to read through the following list of self-care suggestions and pay particular attention to those things that you are doing regularly and those you are not, and then please DO THEM! I don't mean to shout, but I know only too well how totally devastating burnout is, and what it can do, not only to you personally, your future, your dreams, your beautiful body, your energy, your love life, your sexuality, your ability to make the most of your remarkable talents and uniqueness, but also to those around you who love you.

Some of these ideas may sound strange if you're not accustomed to listening to the inner wisdom of your body, but I assure you they have been tried and tested, and if you find you need to satisfy any scepticism, you'll discover that much scientific research has found them to be effective.

So for now I want you to be totally selfish as it is only by being selfish that you become *un*selfish. You can't be a Feminine Leader if your cup isn't overflowing. It is only from that place of nourishment and self-care that you can live fully and give fully.

Give yourself permission to do the following:

1. *Take at least one hour a day and one day a week to do what YOU
    want to nourish your body and your soul* – Most people when I
    say this to them tell me they haven't got the time to do that, but
    believe you me, you haven't got time to be ill, wiped-out, unable
    to lift your head from the pillow and feeling so drained that you
    wonder if you'll ever recover! So this is priority – you can take it in
    smaller chunks if necessary, but ideally, go to where your pleasure
    lies. I'm not talking about going shopping or going to the pub or
    going on-line. It may be for a swim or a massage or browsing in a
    book shop, or surrendering to the delicious sights and perfumes in
    a flower shop, for a walk in the park, jumping in puddles, reading
    some chapters of a novel, absconding for an afternoon girly film at
    the cinema, walking through the bluebells, bubbling away in a hot
    tub, visiting a cathedral, listening to a concert, singing in a choir,
    going to an art gallery, a train journey through the countryside,
    lying on a beach, rowing a boat on the lake, or painting a picture,
    just for fun.

Whatever you choose, make sure it's for *your* benefit – not the children or
the family or your partner or work, but to inspire and uplift *you*. Ideally
do this on your own, then you have no one else to concern yourself with,
no one else's opinions or desires to consider.

Simply ask yourself: "What would be most fun/joyful/nourishing for me
today?"

2. *Dance the exercises in this book* – Put at least one of them into your
    regimen every day. Sadly, we've been dissected by a society that
    views women as separate parts – breasts, legs, hair, nails, vulva,
    bottom, thighs, but rarely as a unified whole. Oriental healing
    traditions recognise a creative life force, or energy known as 'Ki' or
    'Chi' in all things. When this energy is flowing smoothly, health
    and wellness reign. When it's blocked, dis-ease can result. So by
    doing these exercises you're also stimulating your natural healing
    ability – mentally, physically, emotionally, and spiritually.

3. *Relax* – We spend too much time in heightened states of awareness
    and high-frequency brainwave activity. By slowing down your
    brainwaves, you can return to a state of rest and relaxation. By that

181

I mean coming away from computers and television, your mobile phone and reading, and just tuning in to nature. Or listening to relaxing hypnosis tracks which lead your body from its emergency energy of the sympathetic nervous system to the gentle restorative, rejuvenating, parasympathetic nervous system. It's not just your body that needs to relax – it's your mind too. As Gandhi said: "You need to *be* the change you want to see in the world."

Just hoping that things will change is not enough. You are the agent of change. Practise mindfulness or go to a meditation class so you tune into yourself every morning and before you go to bed.

4. *Breathe* – If it's appropriate and if you have the opportunity to play some beautiful melodic music, do The Breathing Dance. This will also take you into your parasympathetic nervous system and restore a sense of harmony and equilibrium. Taking deep breaths is not the answer – you need to breathe with a rhythmic movement, using all of your lungs, not just the top half. If you're not in the right place to do that, breathe in for a count of six and out for a count of nine or similar until you establish a rhythm. Breathing through your nose takes you deeper into the body.

5. *Get out into nature* – Head for the leafy park or the woods, your garden lawn or the beach, kick off your shoes if possible and connect with the earth. Allow yourself to be grounded, by sending all the unnatural electricity that has built up in your body down into the earth. This is like unplugging from the mains, and allowing your body to just *BE*.

    If possible, lie down on the grass and rest there for a few moments, imagining roots coming from your body down to the centre of the earth, wrapping themselves around the healing rocks and gemstones that lie beneath. Your skin also needs 20 minutes of sunshine on it a day to build up vital vitamin D reserves – we have become so obsessed with slavering on chemicals to protect our skin that we are now suffering from depleted D vitamins. So wherever possible, bask in sunshine if appropriate.

6. *Find movement and exercise that you enjoy* – The secret for accessing energy at any time whenever you want it is to just *move!* If you hate the gym, then you're not doing your body any good at all

by forcing yourself to go there. If this is the case, find something you love to do, and go and do it. It may be flamenco, salsa, belly dancing, walking or trampolining, horse riding or skiing, playing tennis, hula hooping, swimming, rolling in buttercups or walking across the fields. Whatever it is, make sure it's something that nourishes body, heart and soul for you and not just endlessly pumps up your physical body. Anything that helps stimulate your body's energy flow, strengthen your muscles and reduce fatigue is good. Take notice of your energy levels and always self-regulate, so if you begin to feel too tired, pause or stop and rest. Don't push through.

Exercise has been proven to be a key factor in combatting many stress-related illnesses, to stimulate the body's energy flow, to strengthen muscles and awaken your vitality and reduce fatigue. But please be aware of the masculinised versions of exercise that can leave you depleted and with high testosterone levels as some aerobic dance/exercise classes are prone to do!

7. *Be the Mistress of Your Emotions* – Start and end your day with positive uplifting thoughts, affirmations or mantras. Thoughts, attitudes and emotions are increasingly linked to health and may be the foundation to your wellbeing. Your Top Drawer Memories give you a way to gain control of your negative fear-based thoughts, and enable you to realise a greater focus and centredness within. They help you to concentrate – literally join your centre to whatever you are doing. Run through your Top Drawer Memories the moment you wake up, when you're in that special hypnogogic space halfway between sleeping and waking, so they will be more easily imprinted on to your unconscious mind.

Read them while you're getting dressed or laminate them and read them in the shower. Or record them in your own voice on to a recording device and listen through your headphones on the way to work. Adding to them every time you experience something wonderful helps keep them alive and fresh. Keep a big jar nearby in your bedroom or kitchen, and write down all the good memories you have as they occur – these may be things you've achieved or experienced, or lovely things that other people say about you, and put the pieces of paper in the jar. Then any time you have a

183

wobbly moment, pop your hand in the jar and pull out a piece of paper with your words on and read them, just to remind you how amazing you and your life really are.

8.   *Awaken Your Creative Potential* – Your mind really does create your reality, so it needs waking up from the normal routines and patterns of behaviour that have settled into your habitual way of doing things. So I invite you to change the way you do things. Start your day differently. When you get up, vary your routine. Do *The Breathing Dance* before you go to work. Shake your tail feather, dance around the room instead of plodding through the beginning of the morning. If you normally put your right shoe on first, try putting your left one on first. If you normally shower from the top down, shower from your toes up – and sing. Move things around in your kitchen; write with your non-dominant hand; take a different route to work; shop in a different town; walk instead of taking the car and explore your surroundings. Whatever you do, just do it differently. Be really creative here so new neural pathways can develop in your brain and open up your creativity. By doing so, you will release self-debilitating beliefs and thought patterns which have been wired into your brain through repetition, and thus release your infinite creative wisdom.

9.   *Play* – Do things you loved to do as a child – reclaim parts of childhood you have lost or maybe never had the chance to experience. Play hopscotch, go skipping, climb trees, borrow roller skates, play Jacks or five-stones, play cat's cradle with a piece of string, do French knitting, bake biscuits, make up stories and write them down, splash around with paints with no outcome other than just the fun of putting paint on to paper. One of the joys of having children (or borrowing them for the day) is that you can play on the floor again. Make camps and houses, sing, draw, dance, play silly games and watch kids' films!

10. *Drink water* – pure water, out of glass bottles preferably, not plastic. I know you know this, but typically we turn to food when our body registers some feeling of discomfort, but more often than not it's just crying out for water. Water makes your brain clearer, helps to move along everything in your digestive system, clears out toxins, raises your energy levels and makes your skin clearer

too, as well as many other benefits, including rejuvenation! Even if you juice vegetables and fruit so that you have a good portion of nutrient-rich water in your system, you still need pure water. To get down to basics here, your urine needs to be the colour of light straw. Any darker means that your body is working far too hard to rid itself of toxins.

11. *Eat food that hasn't been tampered with* – in other words, food with Low Human Interference. Women account for 85% of buying decisions so we literally can change the world just by the way we choose to shop! Our TV screens are inundated with cookery programmes, yet go to any shopping store and you'll see trolleys laden with pre-cooked food that is so far away from its natural state that artificial flavours, colours and preservatives have had to be added to make it even vaguely appealing to us, none of which is good for our bodies. While convenience foods may be convenient time-wise, long term they will steal your life-force, your energy and your health and vibrancy.

I love the 80/20 rule. You don't need to be a saint but 80% of the time eat food which is fresh, energising, natural, and, if at all possible, organic. If you look at the price of food, look what you can buy for the cost of a small calorie-rich chocolate biscuit bar – probably a banana, an apple, a couple of tomatoes on the vine and some sugar snap peas. While the chocolate biscuit leaves you hungry and wanting more a few minutes after flooding your system with sugar, the fruits and vegetables leave you feeling refreshed and fuller longer. Life force is vital here – it's the Chi or energy of the plants that brings energy into your body, whether you nibble on them whole or juice your vegetables with a bit of fruit, or make them into a delicious smoothie.

12. *Sleep* – We may not need the full eight hours solid sleep we've had drummed into our heads after all. Recent research has uncovered the fact that our ancestors in the not too distant past before the Industrial Revolution probably used to sleep in blocks of four hours. After the first four hours, they would wake up in the middle of the night, do some chores or read or make love, then go back to sleep for another four hours. This was natural – no one thought any different. It wasn't until artificial light came in that this began

to change. So if you wake in the night, rather than lying there for ages and fretting, get up and do some of these things that you normally would do during daylight hours, but nothing too mentally stimulating. Do the ironing; sort out a drawer; then go back to bed for the next tranche of sleep. To make up for it, you may need to catnap during the day (20 minutes is all you will need) or go to bed earlier, but it will be worth it. Sleep is vital for restoring your energy, your cells, for rejuvenation and for your mind to process information, so doing without it is one of the worst things you can do. I know the temptation is to ignore the feelings of tiredness and just push through, but take note: rest when your body demands it, or you may find yourself laid up in bed for weeks instead, those duvet days turning into duvet weeks! And wear bedsocks if your feet are cold in bed!

13. *Take out all electrical equipment from your bedroom* – in fact make your bedroom a place just for relaxing, making love and sleeping. So no mobile phone, laptop or TV allowed. Switch off and take out all electric plugs from the socket, and ensure your Wi-Fi router is unplugged overnight.

14. *Create rituals* – Rituals are very calming and soothing. Shower when you get home from work to wash away the day's stresses and the energy of the people you've come into contact with. Take a warm bath an hour before going to bed, with delicious scents. Light a candle and write out on paper everything that's in your head before you tuck down, so your brain can relax as you drift off, knowing that your thoughts are all down on paper and can be picked up again in the morning if you need to. Create rituals that work for you.

15. *Make love often* – I'm not talking about casual sex here with anyone who happens to be passing, but nurturing, nourishing, fulfilling sex that goes much deeper than just a passing fancy. If you don't have a partner, then I'm going to ask you to be creative here, but choose wisely who you share your sexual energy with. Also a 'battery-operated boyfriend' tends to be very clitorally focused, which again is very masculine energy and will deplete you. If you can find a G-spot massager for your Goddess spot, you'll release a lot of tension. Orgasm is now being recognised for its health-

inducing benefits, particularly for women, so please look after yourself in this area!

16.　*Find the support of other women* – The way women cope with stress is through the support we find in friendships, and sharing what is truly in our hearts. Just being listened to is often enough.

17.　*Learn to put boundaries in place* – The 'Saying No' exercise is vital here. Saying "No" to something or someone else is saying "Yes" to your own life, your own integrity. Stop doing other people's stuff – ask yourself, "What's the cost to me here?" Practise saying: "Thank you for asking me, but that won't work for me right now." No explanations, no apologies!

18.　*Take regular breaks* – Studies indicate that you do much better when you work for brief periods of around 90 minutes. Walk, stretch, go outside, dance, nap and engage your right brain through daydreaming. You deaden creativity if you don't take a break, and will get far more done in your day if you do.

19.　*Stop doing what isn't working* – 20% of your actions result in 80% of the results that you get. So what is the 20% of what you do that gives you the most results, as opposed to the 80% that drains your energy? Make the former your priority.

20.　*Give yourself time to be on your own* so you have some solitude and stillness, allowing you to hear that still small voice inside.

21.　*Get rid of clutter and make life easier* – clutter distracts your mind and always saps energy.

22.　*Take good quality food supplements, the best you can afford* – Ideally visit a nutritionist and find out exactly what you need to support your body and your lifestyle. Particularly look out for vitamin D, magnesium and the B vitamins.

23.　*Keep a gratitude journal* – Each day record in your journal at least three things that you are grateful for. It could be for your morning shower, or that someone created a beautiful meal for you, or rubbed your aching back, or that you had a few minutes of sun on your face, or that a friend phoned to see how you were, or you laughed at something funny. There are always things to be grateful for, and gratitude brings in its wake a whole host of beneficial events. Appreciation appreciates – the more you appreciate, the more comes your way for you to appreciate! Remember you get more of whatever it is you are focusing on! Gratitude brings a whole new dimension to life.

24. *Watch a funny film* – Laughter really has been proven to be the best medicine. So when you are feeling good, store up a pack of funny and feel-good DVDs to watch if you get low and you can't go outside.

25. *Get some heartfelt hugs* – it is said you need four hugs a day to keep you alive, eight hugs for maintenance and 12 hugs for growth. Many of us are touch-deprived which has an impact on self-esteem and health. Even hugging a beloved pet helps. A quick hug has a near-immediate impact on health, lowering your heart rate and inducing a calming effect while also leading to a more upbeat mood! A full body hug stimulates your nervous system while decreasing feelings of loneliness, combating fear, increasing self-esteem, defusing tension and showing appreciation. However, hugs must be with someone you trust, so please use discernment!

26. *Forgive yourself for not being as perfect as you think you should* – and forgive yourself for your self-neglect. Be gentle on yourself. Recognise you are already enough, and if you have to pull back for a while, allow yourself to do that.

27. *Stop multi-tasking* – As women we pride ourselves on being able to do five things at once, but in fact it means we do nothing particularly well. If you have lots of things you want to do, set a timer with gentle music (not an alarm!) for 20 minutes and just do one thing for that time, being totally present, pouring all your attention and awareness into the situation. After 20 minutes, get up, stretch, move, and then decide whether you want to continue for another 20 minutes or change to something else.

28. *Learn to be present* – Throughout this book I've talked about presence. When you are present, in the moment, your life will change.

29. *Remember your aspirations* – Bring yourself back to remembering what you really want in this life, and keep adjusting until it works for you.

30. *Celebrate the small wins* – So often, we achieve so many of our daily outcomes, but instead of celebrating, we rush off to the next thing. Celebrate everything you achieve, no matter how small. Get to be your own heroine!

Notice when you are off-centre, when your energy is starting to feel compromised. And STOP! Your life literally does depend on it. Your body will only give you a certain number of warning signs before it grinds to a halt. It is your choice – risk being bed-ridden for months, or rest, recuperate and replenish en route.

The real truth is you cannot put yourself last. Putting yourself last is like saying to your Creator (whatever or however you think of that) that what It has created is inferior. It's almost the ultimate rejection of the Universe.

This truly is the greatest love of all, to love and honour yourself. And to recognise that until you do, you can't do what you're here in the world to do as a Leader.

Chapter 20
Conscious Feminine Leadership

Knowing how to be a conscious leader following the Feminine Principle outlined in the book raises you head and shoulders above the majority. This is all about leading by example. When you dare to take a quantum leap, and follow the road less travelled, you'll create success and prosperity in your business, as well as achieving greater balance and harmony in your personal life.

This is the opportunity to make the difference I know you crave, while owning and acknowledging the magnificence of what it is to be a woman in this important time of the 21st century. Here is the chance to dream, envision and actualise your purpose while also tapping into your creative energy.

Earlier in the book we talked about your own personal values. Leadership always comes from within, so it is vital you work out what's important for you first and let go of what's holding you back: this is not about changing who you are, but rather, becoming *more* of who you are.

Being a leader in the 21st century also means reconsidering preconceived ideas. Women typically look for certainty, trying to cover all eventualities, which causes us more anxiety than anything else. But the current business and social climate is so complex and rapidly changing, that it's no longer possible for any one person to have fixed knowledge.

So you need to have an enquiring mind – not one that thinks it knows the answers but rather, one which questions. Open questions lead your brain into seeking new possibilities.

What dreams do I hold dear in my heart?
How can I make a profound difference in the world?
What do I need to know here?
What has to happen to make the outcome better for everyone?
What can I do differently?
What have I not thought of that can make all the difference?
What can I do to contribute to the evolution of the planet and humanity?
Who am I today and what can I bring to the world?

Then allow the solutions to arise – you don't have to chase them. Once you know your aspirational outcome and have set it into motion, if you're passionately determined to create solutions that enhance the world, all sorts of things will happen that may be out of your control that will, as if by magic and synchronicity, arrive to support you.

Conscious Feminine Leadership means being able to communicate well, to be the one that others look up to by the potency of your presence, to be sensitive to circumstances and aware of the consequences of your own actions. It's about being the radiant hub around which others gather.

Leading others requires a certain set of qualities which you can develop, many of which have been covered already in this book: vision, purpose, creativity, vitality, awareness, positive mindset, winning values, appropriate timing, the ability to give and receive feedback, giving others the space they need to express themselves, being open to intuition, being able to listen with your heart, not just your head, and responding, rather than reacting.

In addition to these, leading others requires other qualities as well:

Integrity – being consistent and truthful with your actions, behaviours and the way you communicate, so you honour your agreements.

Individuality – being willing to be uniquely yourself.

Innovative – having the ability to create and think in a more expansive way.

Inspirational – to motivate comes from a masculine paradigm, but being quietly inspirational so that others awaken to what is also in themselves is a wonderful attribute.

Invigourating – to bring Life back into business and the work environment.

Involving – being *in*clusive rather than *ex*clusive – listening to others.

Intuitive – using your instinctual knowing and deep wisdom.

Empathic – being sensitive to the thoughts and feelings of others.

Balance and harmony – giving your personal life as well as your work life its due.

Patience – taking a long-term view and allowing things to evolve in their own time.

Generosity – being expansive with your time, contacts, advice and support.

Accountability – being accountable for all your actions and non-actions.

Awareness – of yourself and awareness of others.

Feedback – knowing how to give and interpret feedback through body language and the spoken word.

Discernment – being conscious enough to be discerning with other people and circumstances.

Self-acceptance – embracing the beauty and all aspects of who you are at your core. Embracing both the dark and light sides – and the dynamic integration of both.

Understanding – what drives us, our values and beliefs, and to learn which are empowering and which we need to change.

Trusting – not blind trust, but trusting that people will be who they are, no matter what, and not trying to make them be like you. Learning to trust in Life.

Clear communication – being able to speak lovingly from your own needs, desires, truth, vision and boundaries.

Higher perspective – being able to rise above and see the potential in any situation and act accordingly.

Self-confident – trusting in yourself, and so allowing you to lead from your inner strength.

Commitment – commit to your own vision and goals – be realistic with time and follow through.

Self-authority – recognising that you are the author of your life – no one else – and so you have the right to make decisions and judgements based on your own needs and desires.

Humility – seeking to serve others and share credit.

Open to receive – embracing the mystery and synchronicity in life, and allowing good things to come to you.

Connected – connecting with that sacred creative force inside you.

Vulnerability – owning up to your limitations and asking for help.

As always, this list is not the be all and end all. I am sure you can come up with other qualities. But for now it is important that you realise you cannot do it all by yourself. *You need others around you who share the same strong vision of the world you want to live in.*

Finally, Conscious Feminine Leadership requires fun, flexibility and fluidity – a willingness to go with the flow and adapt at a moment's notice. You become the dancer of your own dance – true embodiment in the present moment. So much so, that in time you become the dance itself.

It's impossible to step into Feminine Leadership with no basic trust in life. So the more you do this work and subsequent coaching programmes, the more you bring that trust into your awareness as you begin to find and strengthen your unique voice.

At this stage I'd like you to kick off your shoes and surrender to the music and the fluidity in your body. We operate so often from a place of rigidity, yet not only our bodies, but the planet itself, is 75-80% water!

Fluidity or being able to adjust and go with the flow – in other words where the positive energy lies – and to flow around obstacles, is probably another of the most important attributes of leadership.

Big Blue Overture – Eric Serra

I invite you to experience again the Dance of Fluidity of the Sorceress. With eyes open, allow your body to surrender to the softness, gentleness and flow of the music, and using your whole body, move around the room, almost as if you were a piece of seaweed floating with the rise and fall of gentle waves or as if you were dancing through marshmallows. When you let go of the tightness and rigidity in your hips, your shoulders, your back, your neck and your arms, your mind will also learn to release its rigidity.

The more you do this exercise, the easier it will become to find new answers to problems, to adapt and let go of rigid thought processes, and to allow your body to unwind and relax.

Chapter 21
Take Your Partners by the Hand

Collaboration, communication, cooperation, co-creativity, community are vital in this new era into which we're now moving.

Feminine Leadership is not a solo activity. Over the last decade or so, in our attempt to emulate men, we've been trying to go it alone, trying to be all things to all people. We've worked to our weaknesses instead of to our strengths, which has frequently led to illness. And while many women have 'made it' for a while, it has often been at the expense of their health, their vitality, their fertility, their family and their personal relationships. Even women in their twenties are burning out!

Success leaves clues. Burnout too, leaves clues.

In the entrepreneurial field, I've met so many women with amazing talents and so much to offer to the world, but, overwhelmed by the myriad skills which they need in order to get their offerings out there, they remain hidden away.

We need to evolve beyond our own inner glass ceilings in taking our work out to the world and break through our own internal barriers in order to thrive and flourish – and to do that, we need the support of others.

We're social animals. Working in isolation, often stuck behind our computers in our own homes for hours on end, our only link with the outside world being through social media, causes untold misery. The lack of contact with real flesh and blood leaves us deprived of the most important ingredient for our thriving – human contact and loving touch, which is why most of my work is in groups, seminars, workshops and retreats where we can learn to dance both physically and metaphorically together.

The healthy human body lives in an exquisite holistic dynamic that involves every system. Every part of our body is connected. Nothing operates in isolation. All works in symbiosis where each part can't exist without the other. What affects one often affects the whole. Similarly, if you are to be effective in the world, you need the support of like-minded people around you with whom to work alongside and co-create.

Anyone who has ever made a big difference has had some sort of support network, be it their partner or a group of friends or a team or a tribe. It's time to play now by different rules and realise that we cannot go it alone.

We all need partners in order to achieve – people who support our vision, and to delegate to those who are able to take over the things we aren't so good at. We have a larger destiny as women, and need to activate the power of the collective field and pull together to affect change.

What is recommended here is to pull together a dynamic team around you to work on the areas where you're weaker, in order to create a more holistic outcome. There are some wonderful methodologies and systems you can employ to help you do just that, to ensure that you create a good balance of people in your network, according to your own skills, talents, expertise and personality.

When you are doing what comes naturally to you, you're in flow – time passes rapidly but because you're doing what you love, results come thick and fast. However, when you're stressed and overwhelmed, you're out of flow.

There is a tool called Talent Dynamics,™ a psychometric test for entrepreneurs and business people to learn where their natural flow lies. This is about who you are and not what you do. Through its categorisation of talents into eight roles: Creator, Star, Supporter, Deal-maker, Trader, Accelerator, Lord and Mechanic, it also gives you an understanding as to who you need in your team around you for success.

Talent Dynamics™ plays to your strengths. Doing what comes naturally and inviting others to do the same creates a flow in whatever endeavours you're involved with. You will find more information about this at the end of the book.

As I talked about at the beginning of this book, I believe we need to lead the world into a natural harmonious dynamic of the masculine and feminine. Thinking and doing must arise out of being and feeling, or technology with no soul will soon take over and we will be doomed. The truth is that women and men are not equal – we are divinely different.

Women operating with their feminine potency will be far stronger and more capable than when mechanically operating from masculine energy. As more and more women reclaim the deep feminine, then the true leaders of nations will stand head and shoulders above the leaders that we have today.

The more we do so, the more we create the space for our men to step up into their true masculine energy, which is protective and caring. In turn, this will give them the opportunity to delve deeply, to connect with the more feminine values of compassion and love. We need to teach men how to treat us and learn better how to treat them.

A woman in her true power will have no fear of men. She will recognise and acknowledge those who are standing in their true masculine power and operating from that sacred space.

Research is now pointing to the fact that the heart in fact has more intelligence than the brain. The heart is a sensory organ and acts as a sophisticated information centre, encoding and processing information that enables it to learn, remember, and make independent functional decisions.

The heart generates a powerful electromagnetic field in a large area outside the body, affecting and being affected by the vibrations of others in its field. The heart as the seat of emotion, the place for love and passion and deep joy and pain, actually has this ability. It isn't just a romantic fantasy. Your heart plays a major role in terms of achieving behaviour change and increasing performance.

As the world starts to shift in consciousness, we are beginning to see more and more companies veering towards employees who are more heart-centred, working more from wisdom, intuition and emotional intelligence rather than just those with intellectual qualifications. This will become more and more important as technology progresses.

So the model I am suggesting here reflects that move as women will be respected and looked up to for their more heart-centred approach to life where previously this may have been ridiculed.

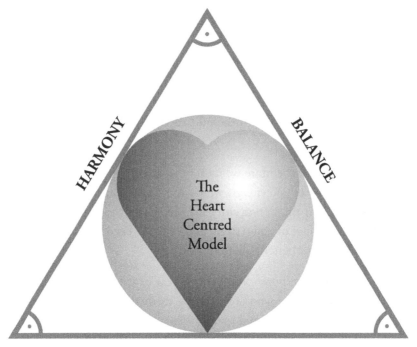

STRENGTH

What I propose here is what I call The Heart-Centred Model. At the core lies the powerful energy of the heart, pulsating and connecting with humanity and wisdom – spiritually, emotionally, morally and intellectually. This heart centre then becomes the hub that pulls everyone and everything that is working towards the good of humanity towards itself.

The heart is nurtured in the circle of the Feminine Principle, representing unity, wholeness, working together as one, no beginning, no end. This is supported on the strength of the masculine at its base and protected and defended by the masculine on the outsides, the triangle representing strength, harmony and balance.

This then becomes the new model from which we can operate, bringing both masculine and feminine in harmony to make this world a happier, healthier, safer and more intelligent place.

My belief – and I know that the majority of the world has this belief too – is that there is something unfathomable and more powerful than ourselves, which goes above and beyond the limitations of humanity. For the purposes of this book, I refer to it as Life or the Universe.

198

Joining forces with this extraordinary power makes us into co-creators with Life. You can employ the wisdom and power of the Universe by making a list of the things that *you* can do, and a list of the things which are seemingly beyond your own ability and power to achieve, and hand them over to that force to deal with. So I invite you to do just that. It may sound odd, but try it.

What I Can Do	What I invite the Universe to Do

Just hand it over and let go – it will support you. This is where we become co-creators with Divine Intelligence. You will be in awe of what and who turns up.

Ask and you shall receive. And when you do so, be grateful for it all, every small thing.

Chapter 22

Dancing with Life

The highly refined, specific tools presented in *Dance Your Way to The Top!* are based on over 45 years of scientific study from around the world. They promote mental and emotional health, inspiration and self-expression, balancing the body's hormones, leaving you feeling energised and creative with enhanced self-esteem. They also remove stress, overwhelm, misery, depression, loneliness and that horrible feeling of being 'stuck'.

Feminine Leaders will do whatever it takes to get their message out into the world. It's an unfortunate fact though, that those who want to change the world so desperately are often those who burn out first. So, in order to avoid this happening to you, I'm hoping you will have participated in everything in this book and not just skimmed through its pages!

Feminine Leadership is about being the best version of yourself, becoming more of who you are and achieving the dreams in your heart, while safeguarding your energy to make sure that you are healthy and strong enough to do the work you are here to do. Balance and nurturing self-care are paramount. Skip any of the sections in this book, and you'll be missing the point.

I have a belief borne of experience that deep inside your DNA is a memory of times past, when we as women were respected, honoured and revered.

We didn't have to work hard to prove ourselves, to strive to be something that we weren't. Instead, we brought to the world a state of grace, of joy, of power, of peace, of healthy connectedness, of playfulness, of strength, of common sense, and of a joyful unashamed sexuality in co-operation and co-existence with the men around us.

You already know all this – you've just forgotten. Your inner self contains the essence of all of you in your magnificence. Some call it Goddess Energy, some call it Feminine Power. I call it Feminine Essence.

History has taught us over the centuries to be fearful, to lose our connection with the greatest feminine energy of all: the earth and her abundance. Politics, religion, technology, the media and our own insecurities have pulled us so far away from our essence, that our instincts have been dulled to the point where we've lost our sensitivity and filled our minds with so much negativity and noise that we can no longer hear, even when our lives are screaming to us that we are way off-course.

And because we can no longer hear, and because who we really are has been so covered up, it seems like an almost insurmountable task to begin uncovering that essence once again.

Physiologically when we're stressed, the spirals of our DNA literally begin to coil up tighter, like a spring, leaving no room for real intelligence to reveal its incredible powers. It isn't until we relax that the strands begin to unravel themselves and our body's natural wisdom has room to play its proper function.

You don't have to do anything – just allow your body to experience and enjoy the feast as you tap into that well of ancestral understanding and claim and own it as yours.

I love the word 'remember'. It re-minds me of (brings to my mind again), the story of Isis and Osiris from ancient Egyptian mythology. Seth murdered his brother Osiris, and scattered his body parts all over the Universe. His widow/sister Isis, in her deep sorrow and love for this man, unceasingly scoured the world to find all the lost parts including that essential sexual part of him, and put him back together again using her wisdom and her magic – she 're-membered' him.

That is what we've been doing in this book – putting together all the parts of you that you've scattered around the Universe, in the mistaken belief that you are 'less than'. And re-creating (create anew) the wonder of who you are at your core, with all your instincts and intuition intact. All these words beginning with 'Re-' are bringing you back to your natural state again – your body knows this at a deep cellular level.

In re-discovering your Essence, you'll discover how easily and effortlessly you can:

- **Re-lax** – *from the* Latin relaxare – *to stretch out again, to loosen*

- **Re-treat** – *from the Latin* retrahere - *to pull back. To withdraw to a quiet place and come away from the demands of the outside world for a few hours*

- **Re-plenish** – *to make full or complete again by supplying what is lacking*

- **Re-store** - *to return to an original or former condition. To restore your energy, returning it to its owner, bringing back good health and good spirits*

- **Re-new** – *to bring yourself to a new or fresh condition*

- **Re-balance** – *to restoring equilibrium and harmony*

- **Re-fresh** – *to stimulate the memory. To make fresh and vigorous through rest, drink or food. To enliven. A mental or spiritual sense of refreshing*

- **Re-juvenate** – *to make young or youthful again. To give new vigour to. To restore to an original or new state. To stimulate. To develop youthful features*

- **Re-cognise** – *to identify as someone previously seen and known. To perceive as existing or true. To resume possession of land. To recall to mind. To know again*

- **Re-call** – *to call back into existence*

- **Re-member** – *bring all your parts back together as one*

- **Re-cover** – *to gain health and strength*

- **Re-joice** *as you re-gain your sacred sense of self*

- **Re-connect** – *to join, link or fasten together, to unite or bind. To establish communication between. To associate mentally or physically. To relate or be in harmony with. To re-connect with your vision and purpose*

Let go of what is 'not you' to release what 'is you', moving beyond self-consciousness, beyond fear and allowing your true self to emerge.

Re-connect to your femininity
Re-member who you are
Re-claim your birthright
Re-vitalise your life force
Re-juvenate
Re-energise your immune system
Re-harmonise body, mind and spirit
Re-awaken your feminine essence, sensuality and sexuality
Re-align to your purpose as a woman
Re-capture the innocence and fun of being female
Re-joice in being you!

I believe we're born with the impulse and inner drive to discover the direction we came here to fulfil. When you are fortunate enough to be able to express who you really are, a unique energy bubbles up inside of you that is invaluable in the world. You are born to make a difference, to become an agent of change for this planet because we as leaders are the ones we've been waiting for! However, you have to look after yourself first – you have to start with you.

Successful women are inspired, not motivated. You need to believe so strongly in what you're doing that it gets you out of bed in the morning, ready to take on the world, doing what you do best, in the fullness of who you are. So don't give up the dreams of your soul. Take a giant leap of faith and the safety net will appear beneath you.

Simply by virtue of you deciding that you are going to make a difference, it's already programmed to happen in the future.

As you'll have seen, leadership is an inside job – it takes courage, conviction and belief to work from the inside out. But when you grasp the possibilities and jump out into life, and live in the fullness of your highest being, the Universe will arrange itself to support your new adventures through life.

Often we give away a large percentage of ourselves just to survive. My aim within this book has been to help you regroup your energy, your sense of self, your confidence and self-esteem, so that you can step out into the world as a fully integrated woman, expressing the grandest notion of who you are at the level of your being. And as we've seen this doesn't mean you have to wait until you are perfect – once you have done the work in this book, you will be sufficient!

As women, we have the biggest opportunity right now with the rapid advancements in technology and instant communication. It's time to embrace what's going on in the world and at the same time stay true to the inherent human-ness of life. Before long, 3.5 billion people will be on-line, and many of them will be emerging entrepreneurs. As leaders, we have the opportunity, right here and now, to influence these people to make their businesses ethical, safe for the environment and caring for humanity.

So far, we've looked at why Feminine Leadership is so vital today; why the world and humanity literally will not survive unless we do something about it now, and why you, the woman reading this book, have to look after yourself and learn to love yourself fiercely from the top of your head to the tips of your toes, in order to effect change.

This book has been about waking you up to a new way of thinking and behaving, giving you secrets which you can carry with you in whatever field you operate – secrets of hope realised, potential fulfilled and Feminine Leadership transformed.

The masculine archetype that we're so familiar with is only 2,500 years old so our cultural mode of thinking, rich with logic, reasoning, decisions, conclusions, computations, judgements, limitations and criticism is very new in our history. Our ancestors lived from the earth in conjunction with nature, with their instinct and knowing, and we have all but forgotten.

Now is the time for a massive paradigm shift.

We've looked at the fact that continuing on the trajectory that we've created where we've become overly masculinised in our behaviours, thinking that this was the way to success, will not work. A woman will truly be in her power and potency in her authentic feminine but can never be in her power and potency in the masculine.

We need to use our masculine energy when appropriate, because it's important in order to get things done. We can't even bring a baby into the world without employing our Yang energy, but don't get so seduced that you can't get back in touch with your feminine!

Not only is the masculine paradigm not supporting the planet and contributing towards burnout of some of our most accomplished women, it is also setting a poor example to the children of our future.

It 's time to return to the Feminine Principle.

As the Chinese philosopher Lao Tzu said:

"Know the masculine – keep to the feminine."

We've seen how the masculine paradigm of perfection has caused us to think and behave in a way that is detrimental to us as human beings, as we've become more and more dissociated: where being young seems to be the new religion – where having wrinkles and grey hair are seen as almost indecent. And when vanity and the scalpel take over, a woman's history can be totally erased from her face, so she becomes a woman with no history, an imitation of a human being, a parody of who she really is. We have forgotten to honour the grace and the wisdom of many of our elders, particularly women, as science and technology have sought to eradicate so much of what makes us intrinsically human.

In *The Feminine Addiction Trap* we've explored some of the behaviours and limiting beliefs which are holding women back from stepping into leadership in their lives, limitations that have been promulgated by society, by the media and to which we have succumbed as we've torn ourselves apart. Remember, a belief is just a thought you keep on thinking over and over again – so why not think the more positive ones?

The world is continually provoking us into reactions of self-defence and dissociation, and we are afraid of losing our identity. Society is designed to produce fear, and we've bought into it, losing our basic trust in life. My intention is that this book will be a stepping-stone in helping you change that and reconnect you with your instincts.

We've looked at how the female brain differs from that of the male. When you honour and appreciate those differences, and begin to let go of the need to operate from masculine energies, you can feel the immense power of the feminine. And, as powerful as it is, it has a softness, tenderness and gentleness, with Warrioress energy within it.

In *Unveiling the Masks* you've been able to ascertain which masks you wear to hide your magnificent self from the world, and how to go deep within to find your true self. You've played with your *Inspiring Vision* and danced with the truth of who you are, *Stepping Into Your True Identity.* We need now to align with who we really are – our authentic selves, in order to avoid creating everything using the same old patterns, working with your *strengths*, not your weaknesses.

It's time to stop living other people's lives – no more people pleasing or you won't live your own life. You'll be able to bring much more of you to the world when you do that – something I believe you have known deep within you since you were a very little girl. A huge amount of energy is taken up making others people's reality more important than your own!

Of course, there will be times when you need to give of yourself, but this whole idea of serving the world does not serve you, as it makes a servant of you rather than allowing you to share your talents and skills with the world. This is where your contribution thrives, through you being your authentic self with no dispiriting energy attached.

Rather than living in the story (which is only ever a version of the truth), you've also discovered, in *Becoming Mistress of Your Mind*, that you can rewrite your story, as this is the way the mind works. The mind creates and generates according to the input of information, so when you put in successful, happy content, the reticular activating system in your brain will focus on that which is good and successful, so you can express yourself from a place of joy and effortlessness rather than a place of hard work and misery.

We've also discovered that just trying to use our minds to effect change is simply not enough, and that our amazing *bodies* actually hold the key to transformation and change. The body is the place of a true perception of life.

Yet we've learned to override its messages. Centuries of disregard, of moving away from perceiving, knowing, being, as we've operated out of insecurity and lack of understanding of our own femininity, have hypnotised us into becoming second-rate men. Now too it appears we are moving into a future of dematerialising reality with our use of mobile phones, computers and robotic technology, with terrifying consequences.

What we've been doing is distracting ourselves as we still see evidence that things are wrong with us – we've been trying so hard to change, but that hasn't worked properly, either. We need a way of bringing parts of us into deeper relationship with each other in order to transform the feeling held deep in our bodies, a more holistic and integrated way, which is where the body and *Dancing With Life* steps in. It's not about intellect. A quantum leap is needed here.

In the exercises in this book, you've learned embodied presence – bringing all of who you are to the moment, holding clarity and focus and presence, while being true to your authentic self.

The body is the GPS of divine guidance that is always with you. Divine intelligence transmits itself to blossom in our consciousness when we are open to listen. Your body is not created by you – it is a creation of the cosmos. So when we tap into it and enter into a process of self-discovery using the genius of the body, authenticity (which is not related to society or to technology) begins to emerge.

Here you have access to your innate emotional intelligence, as well as memories that are stored in the cells of your body. So often, we try to gain access to our creativity by sitting quietly, yet hidden within *movement* is a phenomenal treasure-house of untapped ideas and abilities, together with many limiting beliefs we hold which we may not have been aware of before, that may be preventing us from living a life we love and loving the life we live.

Your body only needs one bad memory of abuse, ridicule, insecurity or lack of self-esteem before it covers itself up with shame, inhibition or self-consciousness. So here we are learning to overwrite those disempowering programmes with new memories.

Through moving our bodies with the exercises here in this book, and *Dancing With The Archetypes* of Warrioress, Lover, Mother, Sorceress and Sovereign, we've started to tap into our DNA and 'remembered' who we are as powerful loving women, having deep inside us the qualities needed for true leadership. While men sit on mountaintops and chant "Om," women need to give themselves permission to be wild and chaotic.

In *Dancing With the Dark Side,* we've recognised the 'dark night of the soul' that so many of us seem to have to go through, knowing it is often far longer than just a night or even a few weeks. Sometimes we just have to plunge headfirst into the chaos while that domineering ego struggles to release its hold, and regain sovereignty over love until it eventually surrenders into that sweet spot of authenticity. This connection with one's spiritual essence is not always sweet and angelic – it is more often than not sweaty, fiery and chaotic. To know that that is OK in itself creates a profound shift.

Your body has all the wisdom of the Universe in it – your ancestral energy is stored in its cells, in its organs, in every atom and molecule. The answers you seek are within you, literally!

By *Dancing With Life* this way, we learn to dance with adversity, with resilience, endurance and confidence, with vitality, with creativity and imagination, with passion, with joy and with tenderness. We access those loving and caring, yet vulnerable aspects of our inner worlds, in order to transcend our own limiting beliefs to see what is possible. We learn to cultivate and re-empower the feminine from when we were younger, as we learn to re-parent ourselves.

As you tune into your body, you'll become more discerning as to who you want to work with and how close you want them to get physically, mentally and emotionally. When you tune in and listen – really listen – this can save your sanity. Working with the wrong people can make you sick!

We've learned how the deeper centres below the heart are intrinsically entwined with the feminine, where we store our passion, the centre of our *Chi* energy, which we've often failed to listen to as we've been striving to be more like men. These centres are for our survival, our power, our sexuality and our connection with the earth. This is where our culture has failed us so much as women – we've been training for centuries to *control* these deeper centres rather than *integrate* them with the higher ones, which are tuned into our voice, our wisdom and our spirituality.

These movements and dances also produce serotonin – the Leadership chemical that gives you a sense of pride and recognition of your status. What we've been living with for so long is the highly addictive dopamine, which our bodies produce when we get distracted. Shortness of attention is to do with the addictive quality of dopamine. ADHD (Attention Deficit Hyperactivity Disorder) has gone up 66% in the last 10 years as technology has infiltrated so many aspects of our lives.

If the work you're doing doesn't fill you with joy and a sense of wellbeing, go inside and look for your Inspiring Invincible Vision and don't get side-tracked by distractions. Women are good at complex pictures. We don't have a one-directional focus; we can see it all, so allow the full picture to come into being.

Understand yourself more and judge yourself less. So often, we try to hide the more vulnerable sides of ourselves that are affected by sadness and grief, but this is hiding and masking the real you. Honour and celebrate your unique capacity to feel deeply, to love with uninterrupted focus and to cherish the connection with your environment.

After reading the chapter on *Radical Self-Care*, I trust you've made an agreement to look after yourself, to work out which situations, people, activities and environments damage and do not enhance your mental and physical health.

Be willing to let go – release what no longer serves you, your creation or your work.

There are so many things I wanted to do with my life, so much I wanted to create, yet when I look back, I have actually satisfied so many areas of them at a certain level, even if they don't look exactly like my original vision. There is grace and peace in letting go, in allowing wisdom greater than ourselves to take over where our own minds have created limitation.

I urge you now to take a quantum leap. The world really does need you as a powerful Feminine Leader, as you learn more and more to trust the wisdom of your body, the intelligence of your heart, the knowing of your divine feminine.

This is Leadership with Love – the most important aspect of all, employing compassion and joy and health and wellbeing. It is beyond price.

I ask you too to share the second chapter *Invitation to the Men* with every man you come into contact with – your brothers, your lovers, your partners, your sons, your colleagues, your bosses – and invite them to step up to help us along the way; to champion us to change the world. We need them alongside.

Thank you for joining me in the dance. I deeply honour your courage and your determination to help lead us out of the chaos.

It's time to stop hiding away and dance as though *everyone* in the world is watching. To dance *your* brilliance – no one else's, just yours! The one thing that you have is the uniqueness of you – your special gifts, your talents, your skills, your voice, your thoughts, your body, your abilities, your imagination and your creativity. So sing and draw and dance and paint and build and sculpt and create and write and cook and plan and play and laugh and love and rejoice!

Please bring *you* and share *you* with the world.

Dance and Live as only you can.

What Next?

After reading this book, you may decide you want to delve more deeply into Feminine Leadership to make that vital difference in the world, together with like-minded women, or working one-on-one with me personally.

I regularly host workshops, webinars and training courses for businesses and aspiring leaders, as well as private bespoke VIP days for executives and CEOs where you will learn more methods for Feminine Leadership without burning out! I also run retreats for up to five people in our beautiful manor house in the Cotswolds in Gloucestershire. www.FoxesManor.com

Privately, I work with high-flying female executives and entrepreneurs in demanding jobs or businesses, who on the outside seemingly have it all, yet are inwardly living lives of quiet desperation, often at the risk of their mental and physical health and wellbeing.

They typically come to me because they are exhausted at playing a role that is not who they really are; frustrated about their lack of deep meaningful relationships, with intimacy problems, suffering from low self-esteem and often on the verge of burnout. Sometimes it is because they are not fulfilled and are feeling disappointment, depression, deep dissatisfaction and what

I have described in my book as Feminine Addictions. Once in a while I see people who have fertility issues.

Recently I worked with a senior executive who wanted a promotion but was struggling with personal issues, deep fatigue and on her way to burnout. After working with me for several weeks, she shed over a stone in weight which had been troubling her, joyfully found a new loving and supportive relationship, rebalanced her hormones, discovered how to use her talents and abilities to do the work she really loved, and was able to speak up for herself in ways she hadn't managed before. And yes, she got the promotion she wanted. I don't suppose that applies to you or someone you know does it?

Call me or email me to see how I can help you to live a life of fulfilment, ease and authenticity while being a leader in your chosen field.

Contact Susie: Susie@susieheath.com

www.DanceYourWayToTheTop.com

LinkedIn: Susie Heath

Follow me on Twitter @susieheath

Facebook – Dance Your Way to the Top!

Also on Facebook – the Essence of Womanhood

Special 20% off Talent Dynamics Profile Test

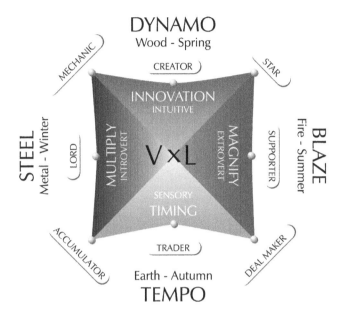

Learn how to play to your strengths by living life in 'Flow' – using your natural talents to do the work you love to do.

Special 20% off price on Talent Dynamics Profile test for all readers of

'Dance Your Way to the Top! – Feminine Leadership Without Burning Out,' by Susie Heath

plus **every sale generates a donation to Susie's charities**

including

Fifth World Conference for Women

http://www.sylviabaldock.com/special-20-off-talent-dynamics-profile-test/

Other Publications

Women - have you forgotten who you are?

Ever wish you had an instruction manual for yourself? Feel there is part of you missing? Spent years battling your way up the ladder in the corporate market or being chauffeur, decorator and general skivvy bringing up your children?

The Essence of Womanhood – re-awakening the authentic feminine

is the book you've been waiting for.

It reveals many essential answers about love, life, your body and feeling like a natural woman.

Available from www.amazon.co.uk

Little Gems – available as a free download from www.susieheath.com

Written in the Rainbow –
A Woman's Secret to Self Esteem

By Almira Ross and Susie Heath

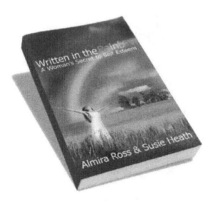

If you're overstretched trying to be all things to all people, and secretly feel you're still not good enough, this could be the most important book you ever read. In it you'll find the secrets to building lasting confidence and self-esteem. The greatest secret of all is that healthy self-esteem doesn't come from reading, but from doing. That's why Almira Ross and Susie Heath have structured this book as a series of exercises, which enable you to develop a strong, valued and exquisitely feminine sense of yourself.

Available from www.amazon.co.uk

About the Author

Susie Heath works with high-achieving executives, both men and women, particularly in the area of male/female dynamics in the workplace, communication and influence, and with relationship and intimacy issues. Best selling author of *The Essence of Womanhood – re-awakening the authentic feminine*, author of *Little Gems*, *The Potency of the Feminine in Business*, and co-author of *Written in the Rainbow – a woman's secret to self-esteem*, she is a qualified Executive Coach, Life Strategist, Relationship and Intimacy Coach, Clinical Hypnotherapist with NLP, Biodanza teacher and facilitator and Corporate Psychotherapist focusing on stress. She is an International Speaker and facilitator of workshops, both in the corporate and private sectors, using the power of verbal language, movement and body language, mind technology and coaching, and is passionate about presence, creativity, communication and cooperation. She recently hosted her own weekly Radio Show *The Essence* for 18 months.

Rather than promoting assertiveness training and the empowerment of women, Susie encourages women to explore and embrace the true potency and intrinsic strength and presence of their feminine energy, and how to apply this in their personal and professional lives. She also teaches Conscious Feminine Leadership, creating and establishing a new way of working which is more balanced and in harmony with the environment and the future of the planet.

Susie specialises in working with professional women between the ages of 29 and 55, particularly in the corporate market, who are stressed, overwhelmed, exhausted and who have overadapted to a more masculine way of being, as well as women entrepreneurs who want to create a more fulfilling and balanced life by developing confidence as a woman.

Previous clients include executives from BP, KPMG, Nat West, Credit Suisse and senior HR consultants. She has run workshops for WIBF (Women in Banking and Finance) and has worked with high-profile film stars, opera singers, pop stars and even royalty.

Susie is a trained TV presenter and has recently been featured on several radio programmes internationally and in a television programme on divorce called *What Would Sharia Do?*

Susie is currently co-creating and co-presenting *The One Woman Conference* with Dr. Joanna Martin and Annie Stoker.

Background

Formerly a French teacher, buyer and designer for a well-known high street store, and later working with Merrill Lynch and Illustra Film Production Company. While bringing up her children, Susie established a name for herself as owner/director of a conservatory interior design and horticulture company Gardens Under Glass, was a frequent TV and radio guest, a TV presenter and well-known speaker for the Royal Horticultural Society. In 1999, Susie qualified as one of the first Life Coaches in the UK, and has since qualified in many Coaching areas, is Coach the Coaches qualified, is qualified in music and dance therapy, and has developed several successful and innovative businesses.

Please visit www.susieheath.com

Please feel free to email Susie at susie@susieheath.com

Linked In – Susie Heath

Twitter: @susieheath

Lightning Source UK Ltd.
Milton Keynes UK
UKOW07f2037300615

254368UK00003B/226/P